ANNE SEXTON

SUNY series, Feminist Theory in Education

Madeleine R. Grumet, *editor*

ANNE SEXTON

Teacher of Weird Abundance

Paula M. Salvio

With a Foreword by Madeleine R. Grumet

STATE UNIVERSITY OF NEW YORK PRESS

Published by
STATE UNIVERSITY OF NEW YORK PRESS,
ALBANY

For information, address
State University of New York Press
194 Washington Avenue, Suite 305, Albany, NY 12210-2384

Production by Kelli Williams
Marketing by Michael Campochiaro

Library of Congress Cataloging-in-Publication Data

Salvio, Paula M.
    Anne Sexton : teacher of weird abundance / Paula M. Salvio ; foreword by
Madeleine R. Grumet.
        p. cm. -- (SUNY series, feminist theory in education)
    Includes bibliographical references and index.
    ISBN-13: 978-0-7914-7097-8 (hardcover : alk. paper)
    ISBN-13: 978-0-7914-7098-5 (pbk. : alk. paper)
        1. Sexton, Anne, 1928–1974.   2. Poets, American--20th century--
Biography.   3. Women educators--United States--Biography.   4. Education--
Philosophy.   5. Education--Social aspects.   I. Title.
PS3537.E915Z84 2007
811'.54--dc22
[B]   2006023864

10   9   8   7   6   5   4   3   2   1

For Lily, Alexandra,

and Fiona Cass

Contents

Foreword

In the United States alone, there are more than three million public school teachers and over one million higher education faculty performing the daily work of teaching. There are plenty of books about teaching, prescriptive, analytic, telling us all over and over what to do and how to do it. And yet there are just a few autobiographies and even fewer biographies of teachers that try to name and understand the meaning of what we do: hardly any that address the complicated projects of teaching, exploring how a distinct and specific personality uses pedagogy to bring, as Salvio puts it, what she doesn't know about what she knows to a conversation with students. The presence of this beautiful book illuminates the shocking absence of others of its kind. Perhaps Paula Salvio has created a new genre of literature in educational studies, a form that combines biography and autobiography as it studies what it means to teach.

And think about what we do. Every day we leave our kitchens, coffee cups on the counter, maybe kids on the bus already, the dog outside, and grab a train or drive to schools where we talk to other people's children about their lives in the world. For those of us who have made teaching our live's work, we know that if we could string together a text of all those teaching words spoken to students across the years, we would read a kind of story of our lives, expressed in what we said or didn't say about the world, expressed in what we asked and what we told, in what we showed and what we did.

For so long I have wondered about this stillness that blankets the exciting and difficult, revelatory and tumultuous work of teaching. I have envied psychoanalysts who gather together at conferences to study in detail, not only a client's utterances, but their own, understanding that whatever has transpired under the title of therapy is constructed from what both client and analyst have found speakable and unspeakable. I have wished that we, teachers, could study our work together in that degree of specificity and undefendedness.

In her introduction to this book, Paula Salvio addresses the inhibitions that have exiled studies of teaching from this kind of probing inquiry. She notes how normative our field is, how we channel our knowledge and thoughts and communications into streams of "rationality" and "emotional reliability" in schooling. Repeatedly, teachers are urged to adopt "best practices," in slavish imitation of some sanctioned instructional strategy that comes with a warranty from the manufacturer. The presence and individuality that are the markers of inspired and inspiring teachers are expunged from the protocols that regulate teaching, and in their absence other terms are borrowed from law or medicine or corrections to describe this profession. But this is not a book that rushes for cover under these related but somewhat irrelevant discourses; it stays with the discourses that address what it means to know and to share this knowledge with others: literature, history, psychoanalysis, philosophy. In this book, Paula Salvio stays with the problems and issues particular to Anne Sexton's work as a teacher. She studies relationships among Sexton's knowledge of how to write poetry, her history as a student and a parent, her friends and critics, and as she moves among this gathering she raises up issues of pedagogy that were Sexton's and are Salvio's and ours. So while this book would have been an important contribution to a literature about knowledge and teaching, sharing the shelf with Lionel Trilling, Gilbert Highet, Martin Buber, or Sylvia Ashton-Warner, with Maxine Greene, Wendy Atwell-Vasey, Jonathan Silin, or Deborah Britzman, at this moment of scripted curriculum, as administrators and teachers cower under the accusatory glare of NCLB (No Child Left Behind), this candid and compassionate study of teaching reconnects us to the dignity of our work.

Many years ago, when I started my graduate work in the 1970s, I carried images of teaching into my studies. There was one of a long-legged boy, sitting in the last seat of the row in my poetry class, his chair tilted back, his legs in the aisle, knees bent, heels down, feet raised against Wordsworth and me. There were others—the mother who described her daughter to me as a cheat and a thief, throwing those words into the gulf that repudiated and abandoned her desperate child; and all the guilty evenings after I had turned in the grades, wishing that I could grab the sheet back from the registrar and weigh and measure and waver all over again, changing this A– to A, this B– to C+. Writing *Toward a Poor Curriculum* with William Pinar, we provided rationales and methods for wrenching the study of teaching out of the technical discourses that held it hostage then and returning it to its cultural and social, psychological and political intentions. At that time, we argued for autobiographical narrative as a form that could express the complexity of teaching, the way it is rooted in personal and social history, the way it gathers up our hopes and relentlessly requires us to play out the compelling issues of our lives in classrooms, day after day. Each of the methods we suggested involved a form of distancing from the story told, so that we might see how the ways that we constructed this work of teaching were saturated with past experience, ideology, personal desire, and self-justification. It was the analytic reading of these narratives that generated the most information. In choosing to make the teaching life of Anne Sexton the figure of this study, and her own autobiographical associations part of the analytic background of her interpretation, Paula Salvio has created a remarkably generative form for the analysis of teaching and curriculum. Taking the work of this brilliant poet as one instance of teaching, Salvio reveals the links that connect Sexton's teaching to the rest of her life. And as she explicates these themes of loss and reparation, narcissism and courage, she situates them as well in social history and psychoanalytic theory.

The last thirty years have seen the development of this discourse, utilizing philosophy, literary criticism, psychoanalysis, and critical theory in studies of teaching. Some of these works have been published in this series, Feminist Theory in Education, that I started editing for SUNY Press in the late 1980s, and I thank SUNY Press for its recognition and support of this work. Many of these studies were about teaching as their authors studied pedagogy as it related to gender, to history and politics, and to the world with all its materiality and urgency, to families, and fantasies, wars, and ecology and ethics.

As the last book in this series, *Anne Sexton: Teacher of Weird Abundance* brings the project of the series to full realization. When Paula Salvio fuses worldliness to the specificity of one teaching assignment created by one teacher for the students she met on one autumn day in a Colgate classroom, she creates a form that can hold the full sweep of curriculum theory. And as I reread this manuscript, I find myself leaving the text as my mind travels to memories of my teaching life and the world it came from and the world it constructs as the author turns the figure of this irrepressible poet/teacher round and round, questioning her, defending her, criticizing her, recognizing her. As Paula Salvio travels back and forth between the specificity of Anne Sexton's work and the culture of the 1950s, psychoanalytic theories and issues of contemporary schooling and teaching, she acknowledges the performance of living that is teaching, its temporality, its situatedness, its courage, and its poignancy. It will take more than this one brave book to reclaim teaching from its intimidated and guilty silences, but as Paula Salvio acknowledges her own implication in these stories that she tells about someone else, she engages us all in a serious and revelatory conversation about teaching.

MADELEINE R. GRUMET

Acknowledgments

The memory of acknowledgments can never remember well enough the gifts to be recognized. It can never entirely express the gratitude and indebtedness from which any work is composed. The memory of acknowledgments provokes us to recall that the solitude of work has nothing to do with being alone. Conversation, patience, and digressions were very much a part of writing this book.

I want to thank Toby Gordon and Lad Tobin, both of whom have seen me through "bedlam" and back, both of whom have patiently read and reread drafts of this manuscript, and who urged me on with their intellect and unfailing friendship. For conversations about this project in the early years, I thank John Erni, Mary Rhiel, Rachael Trubowitz, Diane Freedman, Susan Franzosa, Ann Diller, Barbara Houston, Tom Newkirk, and Wynona Hubrecht. David Bleich helped me to pursue difficult questions about my relationship to Anne Sexton and how her teaching life has impacted my own. Throughout this project, Dennis Sumara and Wendy Atwell-Vasey have offered the rare gift of intellectual generosity. Their keen readings of this work have resulted in a finer, more detailed analysis.

Deborah Britzman, Alice Pitt, John Lofty, Jonathan Silin, Patti Lather, Susan Florio-Ruane, Joanne Pagano, Bruce Berlind, and Janet Miller have each influenced this work through their scholarship. Gail Boldt supported my analysis through her untiring critical comments. Bruce Berlind met with me during the start of my research, and I am endebted to him for discussing his memories of Anne Sexton with me, and for the range of materials he so generously gave me access to. Gratitude also goes to Chris Leverich for extended conversations and insights.

As doctoral students at the University of New Hampshire, Jennie Marshall, Terry Moher, Barbara Tindall, and Amy Zenger have engaged and challenged me in ways that strengthened my analysis of Sexton's experience as a student of John Holmes.

I am also indebted to my colleagues in the Department of Education at the University of New Hampshire, Mike Andrew, Joe Onosko, William Wansart,

John Hornstein, who have each provoked me, in their own ways, to patiently work through what it means to be a good teacher, and to cultivate in our students both intelligence and imagination.

I gratefully acknowledge the support of Burt Feintuch and Jennifer Beard at the University of New Hampshire Center for the Humanities, and Marilyn Hoskin, Dean of the College of Liberal Arts. The Gustafson Fellowship, a Liberal Arts Scholarship, and support from the Richardson Fund made it possible for me to establish the necessary resources to initiate and sustain this project. I am also grateful to Linda Briscoe-Meyers, Curator of Photographic Collections at the Harry Ransom Humanities Research Center, and Victoria Gold and Maria Esteva, Proxy Researchers at the Center, for their precision and patience.

I also want to acknowledge my colleagues to whom I presented many portions of this book at academic conferences such as the American Educational Research Association Conference, the Bergamo Conference, the American Association for the Advancement of Curriculum Studies, and the Conference on College Composition and Communication, especially Chelsea Baily, Dale Bauer, Mary Doll, Susan Edgerton, Mary Hallet, Mimi Orner, William Pinar, Susan Talburt, and Delease Wear.

Enormous gratitude goes to Denise Botelho, Elizabeth Lane, Michael Canfield, and, again, to Jennifer Beard, for their editorial expertise.

Madeleine R. Grumet has been in my life as a teacher, colleague, and friend for over twenty years. Her scholarship continues to offer me insights into the value of posing questions that bear the weight of our emotional lives, questions that we often neglect because they are so utterly familiar, questions that too often slide into opacity. From Madeleine I have learned to be faithful to the half-spoken question, to attend to it and patiently pursue its course.

I am grateful to George Shaker for serving as an important point of reference for me over the years and for offering our daughters such a fine example of integrity and strong will. For her example of grace and intellectual stamina, I thank my mother, Genevieve Bruno Salvio. I also want to express gratitude to my sisters Genina and Mary Elizabeth Salvio, to my brother, Frank Salvio, and to Zoe Gillis, and Una O'Brien Taubman for their buoyant spirits.

This book has benefited most profoundly from the intellectual example, scrupulous observations, and perceptive advice of Peter Maas Taubman, my partner in scholarship and in life who sustains and inspires me everyday—and makes me laugh.

And finally, and most especially, I thank my daughters, Alexandra and Lily, for their endurance, love, and faith, and for learning along with me to have reverence for the shadows and the light.

༃ ༃ ༃

Earlier versions of chapters 1 and 3 appeared, respectively, as "Loss, Memory, and the Work of Learning" in *Personal Effects: The Social Character of Scholarly*

Writing, ed. Deborah H. Holdstein and David Bleich, © 2002 Utah State University Press; and "Teacher of 'Weird Abundance': Portraits of the Pedagogical Tactics of Anne Sexton" in *Cultural Studies* 13 (4) 1999, 639–660, published by Taylor and Francis (http://www.tandf.co.uk). Both are reprinted here with grateful acknowledgment to and the kind permission of the original publishers.

Introduction

Anne Sexton is most often remembered as a Pulitzer Prize–winning poet who, in her poetry, "confessed" the anguish of depression, addiction, and a suicidal mother's love for her daughters. She filled the most tightly wrought of poetic forms—the lyric—with characters and plots about adultery, death, and the myths encrypted in what she referred to as the Gothic New England family romance, spinning haunting tales out of ordinary life in the suburbs. Sexton made poetry appealing even to poetry haters, and performed her work in ways that resonate with performance artists such as Orlan, Cindy Sherman, and Sue Maddon. Like each of these artists, Sexton foregrounds the female body, particularly the female medical body, by making a spectacle of beauty culture, domesticity, psychiatry, and medicine. In her low, husky smoker's voice, standing at the podium in her elegant red reading dress, shoes off, drink in hand, Sexton would lodge her complaint at the misery of American middle-class women, ironically making use of middle-class style.[1]

The bodies described in Sexton's poetry are plagued with disease, feelings of abandonment, madness, and the anguish of losing family, lovers, and ideals. Sexton's bodies are broken; they endure the pain of starving, bloated stomachs (1981, 370), sagging midriffs, and splintered hips; they are "strung out" by the poet, "as if they were still reaching for each other" (23). It is possible, as her biographer, Diane Wood Middlebrook suggests, to read Sexton's complete work of poetry as a narrative—an autobiography, if you will—about a character named Anne who was born to privilege in the New England suburb of Newton, Massachusetts, on November 9, 1928. She married, had a child in 1953, and struggled with the physical and psychological demands of an infant. Sexton gave birth to another daughter in 1955, only to slide into what she described as "terrible spells of depression." She was agitated, disoriented, and subject to feeling "unreal" (Middlebrook, 1991, 31). Diagnosed with postpartum depression, she took medications and pursued therapy with Dr. Martha Brunner-Orne. Her condition continued to worsen, particularly when her husband, Kayo, was away on business. Sexton was prone to seizing her

daughter Linda and choking and slapping her, and feared that she was incapable of controlling such destructive outbursts. In November, one day before
her twenty-eighth birthday, alone at home, Sexton attempted suicide by taking an overdose of barbiturates—Nembutal, which she thereafter named her
"kill-me" pills. This overdose marks the beginning of the years in which Sexton
fell into a slumber among the constraints of the culture she was educated in,
and the social confusions of living as a woman—mother, daughter, wife—in
postwar America. Eventually, Anne was reawakened by Dr. Martha Brunner-
Orne's son, Dr. Martin Orne, and the "talking cure" of psychoanalysis, a cure
that indeed transformed her into one of the most successful and highly paid
female poets of her generation.

Yet the profound impact that psychoanalysis had on her life was not ef-
ficacious enough to truly cure her. Sexton remained sick. She was often lost in
states of anguish that were horrible to her and appalling to those she loved and
with whom she lived. While she could be enormously generous and playful,
she could also be destructive, and she dangerously intruded into the lives of
her daughters and close friends. Sexton too often turned to her older daughter
Linda for comfort and protection, particularly when she felt shaky and fragile
or when she and her husband burst into fits of violent rage. She was often too
sick to care for her children; she felt terrified of leaving the house, fell into fugue
states, and attempted suicide repeatedly throughout her life.

Nonetheless, despite a serious mental illness that defied diagnosis and cure,
Sexton managed to summon up enough resilience and strength to win almost
all the prestigious awards available to American poets, including the Pulitzer
and Shelley prizes. Before her suicide at the age of forty-six, Anne Sexton wrote
and saw into production off-Broadway her play *Mercy Street*. She published in
major popular literary magazines and newspapers such as *Esquire* and the *New
York Times,* and became a regular contributor to the *New Yorker.* She became
one of the highest paid poetry performers in America and, as Middlebrook
points out, she cleverly brought poetry to public audiences who ordinarily
found it dull.

In addition to marketing her image as poet, Sexton worked hard to secure
teaching positions for herself at a time when it was unusual to find women
teaching in higher education. What often goes unnoticed about Sexton is that
in the face of her continual struggles with mental illness, addictions, and an
education that she has described as anemic—her formal education ended at
Garland Junior College—Sexton developed a reputation as a dedicated teacher,
eventually rising to the rank of professor at Boston University. In addition to
teaching at Boston University, Sexton taught poetry at McLean Psychiatric
Hospital, Colgate University, and Wayland High School in Wayland, Massachusetts. Her collaboration with Herbert Kohl and the Teachers and Writers Collaborative in the 1960s made significant contributions to revitalizing
English education, in part by initiating teaching partnerships among writers,
artists, and teachers.

Despite the substantial collection of lecture notes, correspondences with students, and journals that Sexton left behind, the remains of her teaching life are rarely addressed, nor have their implications of her use of autobiography and confessional writing in the classroom been explored. This book does not offer a biographical portrait of Anne Sexton; rather it literally performs a method of writing auto/biographically in which Sexton functions as an interlocutor, indirectly illuminating the gender, sexual, and cultural struggles that influence our conscious and unconscious interests, our scholarship, and our teaching. Throughout the following chapters, I read Sexton's teaching life as a pedagogic project in which she resists the supposed cures and normalizing effects attempted through acts of confessional writing.

As a teacher, Sexton was skilled at distinguishing between personal and confessional modes of writing poetry. In identifying her work as "personal," she not only addressed those critics who positioned her as a confessional poet, but she also defined her work as standing apart from the impersonality that was championed by T. S. Eliot and continues to influence debates in American literature, composition studies, and education, particularly those discussions concerning the place of the personal in teaching and learning.[2] As Joanna Gill aptly notes, Sexton's move to set herself apart from the poetry of impersonality associated with T. S. Eliot, addresses and challenges "Eliot's persistently influential dictum: his advocacy of the 'process of depersonalization' and his admonition that there should be a complete separation between 'the man who suffers and the mind which creates'" (2003, 33). Sexton continually emphasized to her students that the crafting of an autobiographical *I* is a persona that only appears biographical, but is in fact, as she often noted, a mask, a fiction. Her resistance to the binary logic that divides the personal from the social emerges throughout her teaching documents, in interviews, and correspondences with friends and colleagues.

Not all critics were enamored of Sexton's autobiographical writing. Anne Sexton has often been criticized for using writing, specifically the confessional genre, to act out her personal problems, her own "small wounds," resorting to what critic Robert Boyers describes as "excessive self-dramatization, even spilling into undertones of self-pity" (1974, 207). As noted, the criticisms lodged at Sexton for using the confessional genre to air family secrets provoke long-contested questions about the place of self-disclosure in teaching and scholarship.[3]

Educators such as Linda Brodkey (1996), Gesa E. Kirsch (1995), Mimi Orner (1993), and bell hooks (1994) have likewise raised important questions about contemporary forms of liberatory education that ask students to reveal, via autobiographical narratives and the personal essay, information about their lives and their cultures. These educators have expressed serious concerns about this and argue that the discipline of confession and autobiography are rituals of discourse that require the presence of an authority figure who has the power to exonerate, redeem, or purify the speaking/writing subject. When students draw

on the personal under the watchful gaze of the teacher, no matter how liberatory the teacher's practices may be, students are vulnerable to being coerced into
constructing a self they believe the teacher may approve of or the institution
may sanction. One of the assumptions underlying the uses of educational autobiography criticized by these educators is the postulation that autobiography
is tied to the growth of individualism, thus casting the private history of the
individual student as an entity that stands apart from social life.[4] Such positions
ignore the fact that the individual's growing awareness of selfhood emerges
at the conjuncture of relations between the self and others as well as in the
relationships between the self and social institutions. This conception of autobiography can be understood in the context of "American individualism"—a
common but often taken-for-granted perspective that stresses self-sufficiency
and independence and ties these characteristics to notions of "freedom" and
democracy. It is also tied to the forms of autobiography traditionally associated
with white, middle-class, and masculine stories of success—forms that have
been critiqued by literary theorists such as Leigh Gilmore, Sidone Smith, and
Dale Bauer.

This ambivalence over the potential and the pitfalls of the personal in
teaching and learning has characterized my own thinking about classroom en-
gagements. Questions formed: What does it mean to bring into the classroom
dimensions of our lives for which there is such little public acknowledgment?
Why might this matter? How can we incorporate the personal into teaching
without slipping into demand, confession, voyeurism, or unrefined reflection?
How do we make our classrooms a space for the enunciation of something
other than predictable retellings of socially inscribed stories of failure and success? I propose we turn to Sexton's framing and use of the personal in teaching
and learning. While the *I* in Sexton's poetry appears boldly personal, she in fact
considered the autobiographical *I* as a literary rather than a literal identity. "I
am often being personal," she explained to her students at Colgate University,
"but I'm not being personal about myself." Here Sexton suggests that the personal is already a plural condition.

As noted by Lynn Hejinian (1991), we often feel that the personal is located
somewhere within our bodies and, most certainly, Sexton's body images were
read by her critics as faithful representations of her life history, as if her history
was literally contained in her stomach, her chest, her genitals, throat, and head,
as if her poetry was a somatic reiteration of her body. One can look for our
histories [there], posits Hejinian, and in so doing, "already one is not oneself,
one is several, incomplete, and subject to dispersal" (170). Sexton's incongruous
remark, "I am often being personal, but I'm not being personal about myself,"
pokes fun at, even makes the notion of an actual *I* in autobiography seem lu-
dicrous, particularly when we consider that autobiography is derived from the
dissonance between the *I* who speaks and the *I* that is not a person but a function of language. Sexton was fond of claiming that the *I* in her autobiographical poems was always a partial fiction. By casting the *I* in her poetry and her

composing process as a dramatic persona, Sexton is able to point to the ways in which the identities we inscribe through writing are not only linguistic constructions, but permeable figures of language that are politically regulated and positioned on a cultural field of gender hierarchy, compulsory heterosexuality, and norms for possessing academic style and intelligence.

Sexton's statement about her use of the personal suggests a key principle of American language poetics, or what is often labeled *linguistically innovative poetries*, that is, that the notions of *voice* cannot stand firm as the foundational principle of lyric poetry (Perloff, 1999, 405). My ambivalence about the place of personal writing in the classroom pivots on just this point, that auto(bio)graphical texts do not represent persons but personae, and that these personae are not direct replicas of the writer's or the biographical subject's ego, nor do they represent the writer as a whole and unified subject. Sexton understood, albeit on an intuitive level, that writing is not a direct expression of our subjectivity. Rather, writing is always vulnerable to being unfaithful, thus suggesting that the most reliable way to enter into life writing projects, particularly when writing about losses and anxieties that our culture has not given a space for public articulation, may be through images that cast indirect rays of light on the barely audible but deeply felt emotions that students seek to address. Life writing as detour is both the methodological character of Sexton's approach to the personal as well as my own—and it is a method that I scrutinize throughout this book.

Scholars such as Carolyn Steedman (1987), Nancy K. Miller (1991), and Shoshanna Felman and Dori Laub (1992) have elaborated on the ways in which women write their lives through the lives of others—performing an autobiography that is relational in structure rather than heroic or episodic. While this principle indeed applies to my work on Anne Sexton, I also question the extent to which such a method can be used to hide behind or fuse with our biographical subjects. Drawing on the work of these scholars as well as the writing of Toni Morrison, I explore the implications of fabricating a persona such as Sexton. If Morrison is correct, that the fabrication of a persona is reflective, an extraordinary meditation on the self, a powerful exploration of the fears and desires that reside in the writer's consciousness, a revelation of longing, terror, perplexity, shame, and magnanimity, then what kind of reflexive work do I take up with Sexton?

The approach to the personal that I explore in this book does not promise to lead to empirical truth. Personal writing that approaches a life indirectly and thus decenters the persona addressed is one analytic turn that can offer, notes cultural historian Mary Rhiel (1996), a means through which to assess the multiple subject positions that are absorbed by and circulate within a given historical moment. Given Sexton's subjects—abortion, adultery, cancer, suicide, mental anguish, and addictions—all unspeakable topics for a female poet of her time, Sexton's poetic project might be cast as one that creates openings into what lies outside of the cognitively accessible. Her methodological approach demands, then, the inclusion within the thought process of what cannot be mastered, asking that students and teachers surrender to what cannot be fully understood or entirely apprehended. The body of Anne Sexton represents the excess that cannot be contained by discourses in teacher education, excesses that are associated with an inexplicable, relentless mental illness that defied cure. What I want to underscore is this: The figure of Sexton, as addict, suicide, teacher, demon, artist, and mother provokes profound anxieties and uncertainties in us as educators, particularly if we read her teaching life, as I do throughout this book, as a limit case of an exemplary teacher.

Limit cases are more useful for raising subtle questions about education that resist easy classification and offer a method for discussing when and how the teaching and writing of Sexton operate at a distance from the conventions of curriculum studies. By establishing Sexton's teaching life as a limit case, I pursue limit-testing questions about the place that concepts such as melancholia, personal writing, and progress occupy in education. Limit cases do not stand as representative or sovereign versions of "good teaching." A limit case is a critique of that position and the knowledge and truth produced through it. Or to put it another way, limit cases can function to expose the insufficiency of viewing teaching and learning from normative standpoints.

The figure of Anne Sexton is, in many ways, not easily represented because her pedagogy of masks and apparent self-disclosures are difficult to integrate into prominent discourses in teacher education that call for female teachers to be nurturing. I use scenes of teaching and writing to explore the memories of Anne Sexton as a teacher and a mother who, albeit unwittingly, challenges the normative educational imperative that the achievements of intellectual well-being and health are contingent on the presence of a mother/teacher who is "good enough" precisely because she is able to nurture her children or students. I argue that implicit in discourses of nurturance is a logic of control and anxiety about sexuality that is encrypted in the progressive discourses that shape early childhood education.[5] When females step outside the role of nurturer, when they fail to master practices that enable students to develop capacities for self-regulation, they run the risks of being cast as excessive, irrational, unloving, and greedy. I continually question the ideal of the good teacher, as I do the problematic nature of the fiction and fantasies that insidiously inform education, neither of which tell the whole story about femininity.

Anne Sexton has been a provocative intellectual companion for me over the years, offering me abundant resources for composing counternarratives to those describing good teaching. In *Teacher of Weird Abundance*, I take the image of weird abundance wholesale from an essay Middlebrook wrote in 1988 entitled, "Poet of Weird Abundance." Middlebrook took this odd image of abundance from a line in "Black Art," a poem Sexton wrote and addressed to poet James Wright, who was at one time her lover. In this poem, Sexton acknowledges that her "dense similes" and "improbable associations" offended certain tastes. Sexton writes, "There is too much food and no one left over/ to eat up all the weird abundance" (Middlebrook, qtd. in Colburn 1988, 447). Middlebrook elaborates on the images conjured by the word *weird* by tying it etymologically to words such as *uncanny, magical,* and *unconventional.* The sensations carried by these words accompanied me into the Anne Sexton archives at Radcliffe College and the Harry Ransom Humanities Research Center in Austin, Texas, where I eventually found myself in a disturbing zone, dreading that Sexton's teaching life was not going to be as clear or straightforward as I imagined. I began to speculate why Sexton's teaching had been left so unexplored—and why other female figures in education like Sylvia Ashton-Warner, Jane Adams, and Maria Montessori appear as mere background figures in the canons of curriculum studies. Why are particular figures ignored in education while others are recognized? I've often thought that Sexton was not only too excessive a figure to use as exemplary in teacher education, but too ordinary as well. What educators often forget is that the normal is not the same as the ordinary. The norm signifies nothing more or less than the prevailing standard while the ordinary, the everyday lives we lead, an ordinary pedagogy if you will, one that is opposed to the standard or normal varieties, can indeed be strange, polychromatic, and contradictory. The ordinary fears and anxieties that face teachers and students recede further and further into the background discussions in education; they are cast beyond the pale of the curriculum and replaced with the language of excellence and intellectual mastery, terms that, as Bill Readings (1996) argues in *The University in Ruins,* masquerade as referents without ideas. Perhaps we cling to goals of mastery and excellence because lodged in the ordinary are those intimate truths that belie our most profound vulnerabilities. Families can betray one another, trust in loved ones can be compromised, and life can erupt at any moment into an overwhelming catastrophic encounter with illness or death.

Professional anxieties are too often deemed unworthy of attention. At the same time, they slip into our pedagogy uninvited. What pedagogic possibilities are made available when the teacher's meaning is lost, when the teacher's authority is called into question, or when she falls into depression, feels burned out? What possibilities are made available by the disequilibrium that is brought about by such losses of mastery, particularly when these sensations create the change of scenes that Freud attributes to the uncanny, changes that create confusion about who students and teachers are to one another? What does it mean for a teacher to lose eloquence, to be moved to silence, or to feel overwhelmed by a barrage of stimuli in a classroom, to hoard images during a writing workshop, or to cast her students as just the intellectual companions for which she longs?

As a teacher, Sexton erred in each of these areas. Her enthusiastic invitations to free associate during a writing workshop could create such a flood of images that they caused students to feel overwhelmed, lost, and confused. Her addiction to alcohol eventually ruined her keen ear, compromising her capacity to hear the subtle sounds necessary to craft the dazzling internal rhyme schemes she was, at one time, so skilled at executing.

At the same time, Sexton's students often remember her as an astute technician who focused on methods for revising poetry that called for expansion and amplification. She worked toward cultivating her students' capacity to listen to what she referred to as the "half-spoken image" in a poem. Sexton rarely hesitated to make herself open and available to her students, showing them her worksheets, discussing her own problems and processes in writing, and holding conferences with them in her living room. Perhaps the most vivid memories of Anne Sexton's teaching cohere around the sense of concentration and solidarity she created in her classes, drawing, as she did, on what American poetics refers to as the "workshop method" to structure conversation and critique about writing and revising poetry, mixing and mingling the language of psychoanalysis with strategies for revising a poem. Psychoanalysis provided Sexton with a pedagogical orientation, a methodology, the material means through which to offer her students a more personal, less compliant idiom, (Phillips, 1994).

Sexton has haunted me over the years because as I moved in closer to her teaching life, her pedagogy began to look so ordinary to me—so uncanny, so frighteningly familiar. I grew up in the New England suburbs portrayed in Sexton's poetry. My parents are contemporaries of Sexton. One difference between my family and Sexton, however, is that Sexton had a different idea about propriety, for she used teaching and writing to articulate what was only half-spoken in many of the suburban households in post–World War II America: sentimentality, melancholia, and the fears, ambivalence, and anxieties associated with addictions.

In my own case, Sexton not only provoked me to feel anxious and, at times, fearful that all my weaknesses as a teacher and scholar would surely swell out of proportion, revealing my own capacity for confusion, excess, and anxieties about teaching, particularly teaching writing. Anne Sexton also provoked me to remember my father's slow suicide and in turn to take up a more substantive working through of the complex emotions that surrounded the intersecting events of his death and my initiation into teaching. With Anne Sexton as my interlocutor, I began to recognize the pedagogical methods I drew upon to summon up memories of my father and to come to terms with the vulnerability of the body. I turned to the dramaturgy of the German director and playwright Bertolt Brecht for a method through which to engage my students in a critical perspective on curriculum theory, feminist pedagogy, and studies in literacy.

What I came to understand through my reading of Sexton was that I had not recognized, in my attachment to Brecht's dramaturgy, my use of his rhetorical strategies to guarantee my positions about literature and curriculum. My questions were questions through which nothing was questioned; their sole function was to ensure the validity of a predefined answer. And in this process, I used pedagogy to pursue not a face but a mirror, unwittingly positioning my students to reflect back my beliefs and ideas, my tastes and sentiments, thereby revealing my own narcissistic self-image, an image that was in fact a reflection of canonic culture. Threaded through this pedagogical drama of mine was a melancholic strain, for my teaching life, while offering me a way to make a living, to take up work in the world and hence successfully mourn my father, did not bring me to a mature acceptance of losing my father and recognizing the inevitable failure of paternal authority. "Women," writes Virginia Woolf, "have served all these centuries as looking-glasses possessing the magic and delicious power of reflecting the figure of man at twice his natural size" (qtd. in Felman and Laub, 1992, 36). In this sense, I was not necessarily seeking out knowledge of my students—rather, I wanted them to acknowledge the traditions I brought to them. My pedagogic design was to unwittingly cast them as the intellectual companions I longed for and, in doing so, I committed a dangerous form of self-deception: I believed that what was good for me was good for my students.[6]

What I also could not imagine was how my studies of Anne Sexton would turn me back toward memories of my mother and me. I understood then that I had turned away from the strength my mother possessed during the time that my father was dying. I romanticized my father's life, and this act of romanticism exacted a price on my teaching life. My mother sensed the injustice that accompanies the romanticizing of male individualism.

My mother did not have a formal understanding of the limits of romanticism, but she understood, in a deep and heartfelt way, the dangers inherent in embracing the sort of romantic sensibility that Nietzsche described as "revenge against life itself." When the romantic becomes disappointed with life because the longing for absolute merger is frustrated, then, as Jungian analyst Linda Leonard (1989) explains, "romanticism can degenerate into the cynical, life-denying resentment of Dostoevsky's underground man" (87). The romantic withdraws from the world and seeks escape in ecstasy, solipsistic self-expression, and the unboundedness associated with the semiotic register.

Perhaps my mother was sensitive to the dangers inherent in individualism because she knew intimately how loneliness can hurt, and how individual rebellions are so likely to fail. While my mother had many close friends, her friendships after marriage did not lead her to pursue her own appetites and ambitions. What blueprints were available to Italian American women like my mother, women who had aspirations that extended beyond the family? My mother was not married until she was thirty-two years old—relatively late for a woman in 1958—after she had studied music at Julliard and worked at the Foundling Hospital in New York City tracking black market babies and caring for unwed mothers. Like many women of her generation, my mother worked with other women, young women who violated societal standards for respectability and grace. They were excluded from their homes, neighborhoods, and schools because their pollution behavior contradicted and confused the cherished classification systems of post World War II society. The pregnant women my mother lived and worked with were sequestered in the hospital where they prepared to give birth to infants they would give up for adoption. Rarely did my mother speak of the anguish and grief these women felt, although there were images she still, to this day, cannot forget, images of women slipping into catatonic states, weeping for children they could not speak of and could never hope to care for.

I think my mother put off conventional domestic life as long as she could. Until she met my father—a man who apparently offered her the promise of a different sort of life—a doctor, charismatic, compassionate, and, unbeknownst to her, deeply melancholic, prone to depression and an unnamable sadness that I believe cohered around losing his own mother, my grandmother, a thin, shadow figure in our family.

Memories of both my mother and father came back to me as I worked in the archives, looping Sexton's life in the suburbs with my own life, juxtaposing histories, reading through family estates of shame, social anxieties, and cultural taboos. Anne Sexton's teaching life holds lessons in embracing the strange and unhomely dimensions of our histories without sliding into episodes of self-abnegation. Sexton offers examples of the ethical value inherent in leaving the self open to being transfigured by Others whose company we may have been fearful of keeping.

That women resist the insights offered to us from other women, particularly our mothers, is no longer a startling insight. Feminist scholars and writers have elaborated on the myriad ways in which females repudiate their mother's bodies and the social and intellectual limitations the female body has come to signify.[7] I have most certainly been fearful of keeping company with maternal figures over the years. Or perhaps it is more accurate to say that I have been ambivalent about keeping such company. This is not surprising either, given culture and society's persistent ambivalence about female power, a culture and society that is skilled at whetting appetite and shaming it in equal measure. Female desire continues to be as narrowly framed as it was when Sexton and my mother were raising their children and, to the best of their ability, kept house and fought against and tried to control their own appetites and resist their most destructive impulses, which involved self-punishment and isolation. *Desire* and *appetite* are two elusive words that I have struggled to understand in this book.

My approach to locating *desire* is to take a cue from Peter Stallybrass and Allon White (1986), who suggest following the cultural pathways of disgust and shame. "Disgust," they note, "always bears the imprint of desire" (190). The low domains that we expel as "Other" return to us as objects of nostalgia, longing, fetish, fascination (191–192). Given that exclusion is necessary for the formation of social identity, what education excludes and finds most distasteful are important clues to the forms of symbolic capital that educators accumulate in order to differentiate them from the common and the base. The problem, as I see it, however, goes like this: In education's attempt to establish a formal, balanced, and empty neutrality—as made manifest, for example, in notions of a balanced curriculum or the standards movement—the clutter and mess of the bourgeois imaginary surface. And in education's attempt to quiet the "low" and "distracting" voices through such undertakings as high-stakes testing, it simply exacerbates its duality. In other words, it becomes an outsider to itself—education becomes its own Other, an Other it works hard not to know or recognize.

What is most distasteful in education? Most shameful? What disgusts us as teachers? As students? As parents? Disgust finds its way to the margins of education all too easily, right alongside error, the grotesque, and the excesses we cannot bear such as big, noisy, contaminating or aging bodies, a "strong femininity," and other disorderly figures that exceed the conventional standards we hold for beauty, success, and intelligence. As educators, we tend to approach disgust by avoidance and, in doing so, we avoid confronting what we find most intimate but most opaque about ourselves as teachers. How conscious are we of our need for control, our fears of failure, and intellectual inadequacies?

The indirect routes the chapters in this book make into psychoanalysis, feminist pedagogy, and ethics generate a "weird abundance" of rhetorical tactics and strategies for teaching and writing, raising specific questions about the extent to which our histories—both personal and social—exert their influence on our teaching lives in uncanny ways. These are histories that we not only work hard at forgetting, as the word *uncanny* suggests, but histories that are painful and unsettling and because they are left half-spoken, they haunt our teaching lives. Throughout this book, my interest in strategies and tactics is informed by the conceptual categories elaborated on by Michel de Certeau in *The Practice of Everyday Life*. While strategies are dependent on occupying a proper, legitimate place from which a "calculus of force" can be organized and executed, a "tactic" is a form of rhetorical action that is used by the displaced, the exiled, or persons with minimal access to legitimate structures of power. In spatial terms, "the place of the tactic belongs to the Other. A tactic insinuates itself into the other's place without taking it over. Because it does not have a place, it depends on timing; it is always on the watch for opportunities that must be seized on the wing" (de Certeau, 1984, xix). The terms *tactics* and *strategies* are useful for more fully understanding Sexton's rhetoric—that is, her deployment of popular culture and classic lyricism—in her writing and in the classroom. I use de Certeau's distinctions to elucidate a series of Sexton's assignments and to understand her approach to teaching as a particular kind of performance that parodied some of the most cherished ideals about choice and individualism held by progressive educators.

The anxieties associated with the uncanny sensations that are provoked by Sexton's teaching life are also attached to a failure of memory, a failure Sexton suffered with and that I read as a fear of losing the capacity to historicize one's life. Because Sexton had difficulty remembering her psychiatric sessions, she faithfully transcribed them into a green spiral notebook by hand each week, thereby leaving behind an extensive medical record that would eventually be used by Middlebrook to write her biography. I read Sexton's failure of memory as an uncanny tale about the challenges of historicizing a life by turning to Freud's concept of the uncanny, particularly his emphasis that the uncanny is really nothing new or alien. Rather, it is something, that is ordinary, familiar, "old established in the mind and which has become alienated from it only through the process of repression. The uncanny [is] something which ought to have remained hidden but has come to light" (Freud, 1919, 217–252).[8] The disturbing sensations brought about by the uncanny are attached to not feeling at home in one's own home, a sensation that undermines the prospect of "living comfortably" in the world. This sensation is perhaps best described as feeling strange in one's own skin. Hauntingly persistent, the uncanny is that excess, notes Deborah Britzman (1998, 14), that continually seeks a home—and while it may elude consciousness, living out an unhomely exile, it longs to return, to make its way back to the *heim,* the host.[9]

Such feelings of displacement haunted Sexton at home, in the world of poetry, and in the classroom. She never quite felt at ease in her own skin, and, in many ways, she learned early on to play to others as women of her generation were so well schooled to do. At least for a time, she appeared to strive for the very things that would please others and keep them close. In a 1972 interview with Barbara Kevles, Sexton captures not only a lost sense of self but also a troubling inability to be present to herself or others. She often experienced this when writing, performing her poetry in lecture theaters, or speaking during interviews: "It's a little mad, but I believe I am many people. When I am writing a poem, I feel I am the person who should have written it. Many times, I assume these guises. . . . Sometime[s] I become someone else and when I do, I believe, even in moments when I'm not writing the poem, that I am that person" (1972, 193, 298). Sexton's accounts of her composing process and performances are characterized by degrees of self-evacuation that in turn required that she reconstitute herself daily in the roles she played at home, as a writer and performer, and that in losing the "truth" of herself, she was left breathless, feeling acute loss and emptiness, saying, "I am nothing, if not an actress off the stage." In fact, Sexton goes on to say, "it comes down to the terrible truth that there is no true part of me. . . . I suspect that I have no self so I produce a different one for different people. I don't believe me, and I seem forced to constantly establish long fake and vicarious personalities" (qtd. in Middlebrook, 1991, 62).

The "lost presence of self" invoked by Sexton emanates from the lies that women of Sexton's generation had been told (and have inherited) about the intact plenitude and protection inherent in a bourgeois family—lies that Elisabeth Bronfen (1998) so aptly points out, were meant to eclipse all violence, anguish, and destruction from the privileged image of the family structure. The lies pervading the historical scene at the time were embedded in normative notions of women playing the role of extraordinary mothers and wives, striving at every turn to please the other, consequently committing what psychoanalyst Michael Eigen refers to as an "*I*-anesthesia," that is, the numbing and hopeless paralysis of being able to feel present to *oneself* (1993). This "lost I-feeling," notes Eigen, contracts and hardens almost to the point of insensibility, creating a profound sense of numbness and despair. Sexton's pedagogy can be read as a narrative portrayal of using teaching and writing to mend this profound sense of displacement, both at home and in the classroom, offering educators insight into the sense of exile and displacement that exerts an uncanny influence on progressive forms of pedagogy.

The longings, fears, and anxieties that live out an unhomely exile return to haunt educators, taking form as phantoms, or what Nicolas Abraham and Maria Torok (1994) refer to as *fantomes* or secrets inherited from a person's earlier family history. That the focus is placed on the family rather than the individual history is an important one, for Abraham and Torok's emphasis shifts attention from individual histories and memories to intergenerational, historical memories and complicates easy divisions between the personal and the social. Moreover, their concept of the "crypt," which is a reconfiguration of Freud's idea of the unconscious, offers educators a new kind of psychic topography with which to work, particularly in the areas of reading, writing, and the composing and analysis of narrative. The *crypt* is an enigmatic site that houses traces of memories and emotions that lack coherency, continuity, intelligibility, but call out for full expression. The pedagogical project lies in cultivating the rhetorical authority required to comprehend and give expression to the memories and sensations that are neither fully repressed nor incorporated, neither fully remembered nor forgotten. Thus, the uncanny ushers a particular kind of rhetoric into the classroom that has been described as a rhetoric of hiding or concealment consisting of words—what Abraham and Torok refer to as *cryptonyms*—that conceal unutterable or shameful deeds, emotions, or memories. This rhetoric undermines one crucial ethical obligation pedagogy is bound to cultivate—to give expression to that which our culture has deemed unspeakable or ungrievable—to engage that which we have cast beyond the pale of the curriculum so that it can be properly remembered. The secrets that call out and seek expression are not singular taboo memories; rather, they are tied to the complex unconscious of a generation that might be urged to forget, to forget the dead in order to get on with their lives, even as memories and emotions persist in the form of what Jane Bellamy describes in *Affective Genealogies* as a "crypt"—a kind of melancholia that must inhabit an obscure threshold between memory and forgetting (1997, 22).

Throughout this book I read *melancholia* as a lyric lament that holds nascent political texts that are fused with possibility precisely because melancholia has the capacity to expose the limits of representation and representability—that is, the nonconventional, veiled language of the melancholic can bring about a sensitivity to that which can barely be heard. I suggest that the melancholic strain in Sexton's pedagogy is not simply a personal affair; instead, it is tied to questions that are encrypted in education's social imagination. My specific interests cohere around acts of disavowing old emotions that haunt the pedagogical landscape at the very moment that new ideas are brought forth through learning and teaching. At the very moment that a student may encounter a concept such as pluralism, care, or truth, associations from the past can burst forth in ways that are unanticipated, setting off a chain of emotion and memories. These associations are often referred to in educational parlance as "prior knowledge," and such knowledge is believed to usher students into conversations and deliberations about new ideas. What is rarely addressed, however, is the extent to which such "prior knowledge" can function to sabotage teaching and learning, effecting a "change of scene" that initiates circuits of uncanny sensations.

Grief, rage, confusion, and the fear that can accompany a sense of losing mastery of academic material characterize some of the emotions that surface in the chapters in this book. These emotions disclose stories of failures to lose, to let go, and to remember, emotions that are deeply tied to a melancholic temperament. Because the melancholic clutches at the lost love object long after it has passed on or been worn away—whether the love object is a person, belief, or idea—the melancholic not only refuses to risk love again, but he or she potentially abdicates the work required to forge an attachment to life and to compose meaning. This refusal is made manifest by relying on a rhetoric of hiding that works to thwart, obstruct, and distort meaning.

The chapters collected in this book explore methodologies for reading and writing that have the broadest rhetorical capacities for giving expression to that which can barely be heard. I speculate why such work is important to attend to. Melancholia and the uncanny can be read as vital structures of feeling that offer educators important resources for teaching and learning, for they can function as indices to histories—both personal and social—that we have turned away from or conceal. Rather than working to cure away these strains in the curriculum, I consider how we might draw on the dispiritedness of melancholia and the sense of estrangement brought about by the uncanny to provide insights into our teaching lives.

Sexton directs my attention to the melancholic strains in my teaching that at times steal words, interest, and intellectual certainty. Melancholia has exerted itself on my pedagogy in unsuspecting ways. As I became less controlling about approaching Sexton's teaching documents, less bent on keeping the figure of Anne Sexton at a calculated distance, my relationship to Sexton as the chosen subject of my scholarship became more evident to me. What also became apparent is the way in which teaching and scholarship can unwittingly become the ground on which we may, in varied combinations, deny, act out, and work through attendant issues. I do not believe that we can ever entirely overcome acting out problems. What we can do, however, and I believe as educators we have an obligation to do this, is to check our acting out through the roles of memory and critical perspectives, both of which are, notes historian Dominick La Capra (1999), constituents of working through problems.

Sexton's teaching life might appear to stand apart from the lives of most educators, taking shape as a text that has little bearing on lives in schools. Certainly, when I began this project in 1992, it hadn't occurred to me, on a conscious level, that Sexton and I had anything in common. As you read these chapters, I would like you to consider the following: Precisely insofar as Sexton presents as a teacher of excess, a figure of "weird abundance," reference to her enables us to discern an analysis of the different modes in which education casts the Other as abject in need of cure and, in so doing, fails to come to terms with or, to use a psychoanalytic phrase, "work through" what is most intimate but remains most obscure about our teaching lives. Sexton defied cure, and, in this sense, she presents us with a philosophical and ethical correlative of a situation with no cure or apparent solution and of a radical human condition of exposure and vulnerability. In addition to fracturing the sentimental images of the post–World War II middle-class family, the personae in her poetry, the remains of which are registered in her teaching documents, disturb the easy boundaries we create between sickness and wellness, the rational and the irrational, the domestic and the social, raising questions about the social significance of suffering, illness, and health. "More and more for Sexton," writes Middlebrook, "the problematic will not lie between being insane and being healthy, but within being female" (1991, 451). Middlebrook's analysis of Sexton's struggles with sanity and health as a crisis bound within the parameters of being a female in post–World War II America involves Simone de Beauvoir's idea that the body is a situation.

I want to end this introduction with a reference to de Beauvoir's claim, for it illuminates the ways in which the meanings Sexton embodied (just as the meanings we embody) are lived out and utterly bound to the brute facticity, not only of her sex, but of her alcoholism, race, class, suicidal fantasies, poetic skills, pedagogical prowess and anxieties, and struggles with motherhood. The human body cannot be reduced to either the laws of biology or society—it belongs to both orders of meaning. Sexton herself would not dispute the biological facts of her addictions and mental anguish.

The crucial questions pertain, rather, to the social significance we attach to these facts as well as to the meaning implied in Sexton's resistance to cure. In my estimation, Sexton reminds us that the price exacted for any cure is often tied to acts of forgetting and normalization. Furthermore, we must consider the meaning that we can make of the range of diagnosis that fills Sexton's medical records without casting her as pathological. What impact did her use of writing have on her teaching life? Did her life as a teacher of writing in any way ease the profound sense of loss and displacement she felt throughout her life; did teaching address her insatiable hunger for love and her persistent urge to die?

This book is arranged in interrelated chapters that can be read in any order. In chapter 1, I am in the Anne Sexton archives in Austin, Texas, confronted with a letter written by a student who claims to have fallen in love with Sexton. I find in this letter a series of lessons about learning, love, and mourning that came to have far more implications for my teaching life than I could have imagined. In chapters 2 and 3, I venture to contemplate melancholia at the level of teaching and learning. These chapters are written around Sexton's first poetry teacher, John Holmes, as well as the final assignment that she designed for a course she taught at Colgate University called "Anne on Anne." In each instance, psychoanalytic theory is used to make sense of the historical events surrounding her life as a writer, mother, and teacher in post-World War II America.

In chapter 4, I turn to Sexton's suicidal break in World War II America, a time of apparent peace that was haunted by a half-spoken anxiety about chaos, control, and the compulsion to attain power—all of which continues to shape progressive education. A look at Sexton's struggles as both a teacher and mother expand on the concept of the "good-enough mother," which impacts education's notion of what it means to be a "good-enough teacher." I use these concepts to explore the implications such notions of "goodness" have on using teaching as a reparative act.

In chapter 5, the lack of racial consciousness in the teaching life of Anne Sexton is explored. Borrowing from James Baldwin, I speculate that Sexton's lack of racial awareness contributes to her remaining, on a symbolic level, "forever innocent." The epilogue concludes by way of a summery of the books principle lessons and themes.

CHAPTER ONE

Loss, Love, and the Work of Learning

Lessons from the Teaching Life of Anne Sexton

Depression is boring, I think,
and I would do better to make
some soup and light up the cave.

—*Anne Sexton, "The Fury of Rain Storms"*

The secret must sneak, insert, or introduce itself into the arena of public
forms; it must pressure them and prod known subjects into action. . . .

—*Gilles Deleuze and Felix Guattari*

Long before her death, Anne Sexton meticulously typed her manuscripts and
kept carbon copies of her letters. "She was," observes her biographer, Diane
Wood Middlebrook, "a self-documenting person: from childhood on she kept
scrapbooks of treasured moments; from the earliest months of what was to become her professional life she . . . dated worksheets of poems . . . she saved correspondence, photographs, clippings" (Middlebrook, 1991, xxii). Sexton's many
hospitalizations, taped psychiatric sessions, therapy notebooks, and medical
evaluations also generated a rich collection of data that was, in 1978, transferred
to the Harry Ransom Humanities Research Center at the University of Texas
in Austin by Sexton's oldest daughter and the executor of her estate, Linda
Gray Sexton.

Sexton often hoped aloud that her poetry would endure to offer comfort
and insight to those who, like herself, suffered the unrelenting pain of mental
illness and addictions. The archive of Anne Sexton reveals an unconventional
teaching life; reading the contents of Sexton's archive provokes in the reader a

particular form of melancholia that is associated with a life falling apart, a terminal, unrelenting, inexplicable mental illness that resulted in Sexton's ending her life by carbon monoxide poisoning at the age of 46. After returning home from lunch with her close friend, Maxine Kumin, she climbed into the driver's seat of the old red Cougar she bought in 1967, the year she started teaching, and turned on the ignition (Middlebrook, 1991, 397).

꒐꒐꒐

It is July 1994. I am working in the archives at the Harry Ransom Humanities Research Center at the University of Texas, shuffling through some folders that contain correspondences Sexton exchanged with her students.[1] I'm hungry, restless, and feeling stiff from sitting all day, so I decide to take a walk. Before I leave, I randomly pull a letter from the file, skim through it, planning to return to it later in the day. I note that the letter was written by Chris Leverich, an English major at Colgate University during the spring of 1972, and that the letter is in fact a substitute for the final assignment—an imagined interview with Anne Sexton. In his letter, Leverich details a trail of memories, lost expectations, and emotions that he has kept to himself throughout the term. "In a way, I've fallen in love with you," he writes,

> Of course, it's a fantasy. I know that. Yet, there is something, a force, a charm that is ever powerful and ever attractive to me. So many times I've wanted to be alone with you, to talk to you, to break the formalities of student and teacher. . . . I guess that's a fair summation of my first feelings toward you: an initial sexual attraction gradually honed into a mixture of respect and admiration. As the semester went on and I got more and more into your poetry whole new horizons opened up before me. I knew I was reading your life and what it was to you.[2]

Leverich goes on to capture, with tremendous exactitude, the sense of loss he felt for never having really gotten to know Anne Sexton, noting that the end of the term would mark the last time he would hear her voice. He writes,

> I sort of resigned myself to never knowing you, even after that little spark flared up in me when you called my name—"Chris." But it seemed like only a reflex action after Bruce said it. Still, I wanted it to roll around over your tongue. I wanted you to say it again in your head and remember it. I couldn't stand that you wouldn't even remember my name someday. Like you said in class about John Holmes: "If you leave someone without having them love you, then you lose them." I knew we would leave that way and I would lose.[3]

The explicitly sexual content of this letter can be read as an Oedipal narrative—a son's longing for his mother—and contains images of a desire to be devoured (even if in name only), coupled with the image of a spark of fire that takes hold as Sexton utters his name, a spark that is quickly put out with a dose of reflexive speech. Leverich fantasizes about driving to Radcliffe to meet Sexton's daughter, Linda, where they would talk about philosophy. "But I didn't go. I didn't go because I knew I wouldn't see what I wanted. I wouldn't see a miniature you ... I knew I never wanted Lolita, but Jocasta."[4] Leverich's interest in knowing Sexton is, as he notes, a fantasy that I found troubling. On the one hand, I worried about Sexton. To what extent were the images in Leverich's letter symptoms of his desire to swallow his teacher up, a violent fantasy through which to threaten his teacher's authority and claim her for his very own?

On the other hand, I worried about Leverich. To what extent did Sexton's memories of sexual distress and loss figure into her pedagogy at this time, mixing in with this student's past, a past wrought with pain and loss that he may very well have been working hard to forget? I began to think about how the encrypted memories we hold of violence, lost ideals, and betrayals are acted out through pedagogy, memories that appear absent but take up an uncanny presence in our classrooms.

Teaching and learning inevitably invoke ghosts from the past, family dramas, and failed romances. Nested in each word Leverich writes, in each scriptural relic, is a personal past that was awakened as he sat in class working with Sexton's poetry, among her poems "The Truth the Dead Know," "Her Kind," "Somewhere in Africa," "The Fortress," "Said the Poet to the Analyst." As a student in this class, Leverich took part in classroom assignments that were performative in structure and, hence, directed toward loss. "Give me a persona," Sexton asked her students. "Could you write with your mother's voice about her marriage, about her son ... a woman in church, what is she thinking?"[5] Leverich writes of the sudden death of his own father when he was eight years old, and his admitted proclivity to "look for a mother and father ... perhaps that's what I see in you; a woman who is both dominant and passive, at once bold and timid, and even impatient yet understanding."[6] As I read this letter, I felt as if Leverich had isolated the ache of loss because it was so deeply tied to difficult emotions. Such acts of isolation not only numb pain, but they hold it in reserve, blocking it from circulating in our imagination and in our contacts with other people. The confinement of an unbearable reality to an inaccessible region of the psyche is what Nicholas Abraham and Maria Torok (1994) refer to as "incorporation" or "preservative repression." Drawing on clinical observations made by Freud and Karl Abraham in 1922 of the increased sexual activity of people who experienced a death in the family, Abraham and Torok propose a new category of psychology. They refer to this category as "the illness of mourning." They argue that the pain associated with melancholia is not directly tied to having lost a loved one, but rather this pain is associated with the secret that the loss occasions, a secret that they refer to as the *psychic tomb*. Abraham and Torok understood the flow of sexual desire in the face of death as the final, climactic outpouring of love for the departed. Complications ensue, however, when the bereaved is a parent, grandparent, sibling, or other "nonsexual associate," because, in such cases, sexual feelings and outbursts are personally and socially unacceptable to the mourner; the involuntary effusion of feeling constitutes an event that the mourner cannot make sense of with respect to her or his somber feelings of loss and bereavement. In these instances, the effect experienced in the face of death must be kept under wraps, thereby transforming this final outpouring of love into an intrapsychic secret. The mourner sets up a secret enclave, what Torok refers to as a *crypt*, for the departed love-object, precisely because the survivor is being deluded by society and culture into behaving as if no trauma or loss had occurred.[7] Or, to put it another way, the bereaved returns to haunt the living because they have not been granted a proper burial.

The work of Abraham and Torok emphasizes the ways in which the inherited fears, and anxieties that were unresolved by our descendents are carried into succeeding generations and take occupancy in our lives as memories that are neither fully evident nor fully concealed. This emphasis calls attention to the history of psychic structures, and how psychic traumas and secrets can be inherited rather than strictly tied to individual experience. The concept of the phantom offers us another route into Leverich's letter to Sexton, a route that brings us beyond reading this document as a letter written by an individual student, to postulating that encrypted in this love letter, this failed assignment, are inherited, secret, psychic substances of his ancestors' lives and that these substances can take up an uncanny presence in the classroom. Leverich's love letter might be more fully understood as an indirect, circuitous outpouring of love, not solely for Sexton, as he told me years later in an interview, but also for a beloved aunt whom he had lost to drug and alcohol abuse, a woman whose presence he felt in the poetry and teachings of Anne Sexton. The memory traces in Leverich's writing provoke an unsettling disruption in this class, a disruption that was provoked not simply by Sexton's presence, but by the presence of others who are neither fully remembered nor forgotten, neither fully recognized nor ignored (Abraham and Torok, 1994, 166).

The individual example of Leverich depicts how a seminar space might become a site of private mourning. Leverich's memories of loss appear to circulate and flow through his readings of Sexton's poetry, thereby infusing the pedagogical event with the specificity of his own emotions, history, and desires. We might read Leverich's letter as an attempt to articulate strains of feeling that he associated with intergenerational secrets that were unmoored by the poetry of his instructor. The pedagogical project lies in creating occasions, through writing, talking, and other acts of symbolization, for Leverich to refine an attachment to the half-spoken losses haunting his personal past and to coordinate these losses with the larger social field. This work is particularly difficult, however, when the losses a person suffers with are not recognized as legitimate and thus not granted public space for articulation.

The melancholic temperament that Abraham and Torok sought to understand is marked by a loss of address that gives way to an unbounded state in which a person appears to abandon her position as a subject, for she has no addressable Other—that is, there is no one to listen to her plaints, no one who recognizes her grievances as worthy of attention. In a 1968 interview with Barbara Kevles, Sexton is quite articulate about how writing poetry enabled her to create possibilities for approaching the intimate truths harbored in the unconscious that are not fully spoken, that are, in fact, outside naming and ideologies and that often create a "loss of address" (Kristeva, 1989, 298). Sexton says that

> Sometimes my doctors tell me that I understand something in a poem that I haven't integrated into my life. . . . The poetry is often more advanced in terms of my unconscious than I am. Poetry, after all, milks the unconscious. The unconscious is there to feed it little images, little symbols, the answers, the insights I know not of. (Kevles, 1978 (pg 5), xx)

The masks and dramatic personae that appear in Sexton's poetry and that she drew upon in her classroom hold traces of our selves that we are inclined to disavow, the selves we lose or believe we must lose in order to commit to one life and not another—a mother who gives up her child, a girl on the edge of adolescence, a rapist, an assassin—each persona assembled so that her students can begin to approach the uncharted recesses of their emotional lives. Sexton asked her students in one Colgate seminar, using the example of a rapist, to think,

> What moment of his life would you pick to tell about? While he's having a cup of coffee at Howard Johnson's? . . . Perhaps he eats a clam roll. I myself like clam rolls. But I have more than a clam roll in common with the rapist. What have I ever wanted to take? When have I ever wanted to scare and terrify? . . . If you will look around you with eyes stripped you will hear voices calling from the crowd. Each has his own love song. Each has a moment of violence. Each has a moment of despair.[8]

In asking her students, almost all of whom were male, to locate the emotional contingencies between themselves and the persona of a rapist, Sexton threatens to disband any sense they might have of psychic cohesion, goodness, or well-being. But note that Sexton does not question her students without implicating herself: "I myself like clam rolls, but I have more than a clam roll in common with a rapist." If one understands Sexton's pedagogy as an expression of how personal suffering absorbs and is attached to political life, how the personal is the very place where, as Patricia Williams argues, "our most idealistic and our deadliest politics are lodged, and are revealed" (1991, 93), then Sexton's use of personae can be understood as a means through which to bring her students into closer contact with the aspects of their identities that they may be inclined to disavow.

Sexton offers educators lessons in using personae to address the difficult parts of our selves. Many of the poems Sexton wrote and taught in her classes contain themes of loss and mourning and attest to the psychic and social threat of cancer, early sexual distress, addictions, and madness. Maxine

Kumin remembers Anne Sexton in her early years as a poet, working strictly with traditional forms, "believing," writes Kumin, "in the value of their rigor as a forcing agent, believing that the hardest truth would come to light if they were made to fit a stanzaic pattern, a rhyme scheme, a prevailing meter" (1981, xxv). Sexton often spoke of writing poetry as an act of psychoanalysis that created coherence out of the disjunctive, fragmented experiences that came to take possession of her. For a time, the dramatic situations Sexton rendered in her poetry functioned as an effective methodology for inquiring into memory and grief. In "Briar Rose (Sleeping Beauty)" she renders a searing representation of sexual violence:[9]

> Each night I am nailed into place
> and I forget who I am.
> Daddy?
> That's another kind of prison.
> It's not the prince at all,
> but my father
> drunkenly bent over my bed,
> circling the abyss like a shark,
> my father thick upon me
> like some jellyfish. (Sexton, 1981)

Here, Sexton uses vivid images to convey how sexual assault functions to eradicate identity, "I forget who I am," resulting in a form of amnesia that effectively takes a victim's life, "nailing her in place," imprisoning her, stripping her of will and agency. Throughout the time Sexton wrote poetry—from 1957 when, at the suggestion of her psychiatrist, she enrolled in a poetry workshop taught by John Holmes at the Boston Center for Adult Education, to the time of her death in 1974—she used writing to "make a new reality and become whole.... When writing," Sexton explained, "it is like lying on the analyst's couch, reenacting a private terror, and the creative mind is the analyst who gives pattern and meaning to what the persona sees as only incoherent experience" (qtd. in Middlebrook, 1991, 64). At Colgate, Sexton described the tight lyric form as a cage in which a writer could put wild animals in, a means through which to "make a logic out of suffering.... One must make a logic out of suffering or one is mad." She asserted: "All writing of poems is sanity, because one makes a reality, a sane world, out of insane happenings."[10]

Yet the memories of loss that Leverich inscribes in his letter and Sexton in her poetry do not surface through a sheer act of will. Nor can I simply summon up my own memories and set them in the syntax of an essay. Women, marginalized people, and those who have endured trauma cannot write from memory, argues Shoshanna Felman (1993), for our autobiographies are composed of precisely what our memories cannot contain, or hold together as a whole, although our writing inadvertently inscribes it. While the historical conditions that constituted trauma for a white middle-class woman such as Sexton cannot

be equated with the historical conditions of people who have endured generations of colonization, in both cases the structure of trauma works to obliterate
an addressable Other. Felman finds that memories can surface and circulate
only *vis-à-vis* a process through which we access our stories indirectly—by
conjugating literature, theory, and autobiography through reading, writing, and,
I will add, history and performance, and in turn reading into the texts of culture
our difference(s) as missing, absent, lost.[11] This approach to writing, reading,
and teaching autobiography requires that we are united with the lives of others, not by a synthetic understanding, but whereby one person's concerns are
meaningful to another and these concerns return to us an unexpected revelation, desire, or insight in our own life.[12] The letter written by Leverich was
just one artifact that returned an unexpected insight. As I reread his letter, I
remembered a scene earlier that term, long before I had left to make the trip to
Austin, Texas, a scene that reminded me that Sexton was indeed perceived by
many as a teacher perpetually in error.

THE RETURN OF AN INSIGHT

Shortly after I had received the news that I was awarded funding from the
University of New Hampshire to travel to the archives, one of my colleagues
made it quite clear that he thought the university was wasting its money on this
project. "My wife wondered," he told me with a laugh, "why you would want to
study someone who was not only crazy, but who slept with her students? And
what has this project got to do with teaching and teacher education anyway?"

At that moment, I became acutely conscious of how precarious Sexton's
status as a teacher would be. It is one thing to write about mental illness and loss
as a poet, but to teach in the throes of profound melancholia, anxiety, and alcoholism is quite another. It became evident that the remains of Sexton's teaching
life were quite troubling, because the images that surfaced when I proposed
that her teaching life be remembered, that we might even be instructed by her
pedagogy, were those of a woman in ruins, untrustworthy, and strange. I found
myself defending Sexton. "The truth is," I told him, "Sexton did not sleep with
her students." As I approached Sexton's life as a teacher, I felt myself writing
and teaching from a vulnerable position. I began to loosen my grip on the sense
of command and authority I brought to the archive. In retrospect, I remember
this encounter with my colleague because, as much as I wanted to deny it, his
questions were questions I had harbored all along. The letter written by Chris
Leverich was but one relic that provoked my own anxieties to surface, anxieties
that I had managed, until now, to ignore.

I have since learned that much of what remains of Sexton's teaching life
represents excessive sexual violence, anxieties, fears, and desires to remember
and be remembered, all of which will not remain repressed. To consider bringing these excesses into the realm of education is to threaten the meticulous work
that is being done by mainstream culture: (1) to solidify normative notions of

what it means to be a good teacher and a good student; (2) to possess emotional stability; and (3) to determine which physical bodies and bodies of knowledge are most worthy. Sexton is the symptom that signals the (failed) repression of the infectious, melancholic teacher; she is the nonnormative teacher who is believed by many to lack academic taste and who, as my colleague demonstrated, can function as a foil for educators to declare themselves "dissimilar" to her excessive, tormented pedagogy.

AN AUTOBIOGRAPHICAL FRAGMENT

Anne Sexton appears as an uncanny interlocutor through whom I have begun to approach questions unresolved about memory, knowledge, and the body—questions that were fused into my teaching life from the very start. I began to teach in 1981, the year my father began to suffer with esophageal cancer, a disease that is aggressive and for which there was very little curative treatment. Esophageal cancer does not strike randomly; rather it is selective, primarily inflicting people who are addicted to alcohol. One morning, early in December, after my father had just returned home from a month-long stay in the hospital, I sat at the kitchen table with him, not knowing what to say, yet aware that I had to say something, for he had arrived, we were told, at the limit of his life. And what was left for him to do he had to do alone. "Does it terrify you to know you will die soon?" I asked him quietly. "Alone into the alone," he quoted from C. S. Lewis. He said it felt like that. And, how improbable that it should be otherwise. Long before my father had died, he felt cut off from us, and it was not simply the certainty of his death that made this so. Nor was it the fact that, as a doctor, he knew all too well what the months ahead would hold, his biggest fear being that he would suffocate to death.

My father suffered with severe melancholia that took hold of him at unexpected times, thrusting him into painful silence, isolation, and despair. He drank, I think, to ease an unrelenting anguish that he never spoke of but that intruded on him throughout his life. I could tell you that like many men growing up during the depression and World War II, my father learned to believe that drinking was a part of being a man. I could tell you that like many men of his generation, drinking was tied to rituals that bound people in rites of celebration, mourning, friendship, romance, and religion. But such a narrative departure into cultural history would only serve as a defense against the pain, loss, and sense of betrayal that came to feel so familiar to me as a child. For me, alcohol was never endowed with romantic or sacred properties. Rather, in my mind, it was nothing less than a lethal substance my father used to commit a slow suicide.

How could a devoted doctor knowingly and most deliberately abuse himself? How can a person who excessively abuses himself so skillfully offer others a cure? I was left with questions that I could not put to rest, and for which I could find no meaningful allegorical equivalents or redemptive possibilities.

The losses that I accrued through my father's life and death—a sense of abandonment, betrayal, a severed attachment—are among the encrypted details that seep through my pedagogy and my scholarship.

My father's life and death taught me to be skeptical of knowledge. Skepticism approaches relationships with scrutiny. The skeptic examines events and makes distinctions in an effort to cultivate mastery and see things clearly. Not only is the skeptic determined to avoid confusion, but she is also fond of delay and doubt; she harbors suspicions about forming attachments to concepts, persons, and beliefs. Perhaps this is why the null hypothesis always intrigued me—it offers a method through which to claim an attachment and then delay commitment through methods of deliberate disavowal. The art and science of a democratic education offered me processes through which I could put my skeptical temperament to use. The scientific method of John Dewey subordinates transmitting the past to creating a future that is distinct from the past. This method of inquiry makes precept a function of practice; it exalts variation over repetition, encourages the free cooperation of differences to displace the regimented reproduction of identicals, prefers the doubt, the inquiry, the experiment of competitive cooperation of the sciences to the obedient and unquestioning rehearsals of dogmatic faith that we struggled with in our Catholic household. "One can never know," my father's father would say as he read the newspaper in the evening, sitting on the terrace, drinking a glass of wine.

But the truth is that the feelings of skepticism that flooded our home were more akin to a kind of wholesale mood of exaggerated distrust and an unexpressed yearning not to repeat the past than they were to the disciplined forms of scientific inquiry that my father found so compelling. I could write a narrative history of my family's skepticism for you. I could write about the ambivalence my paternal grandfather felt about educating his children—skeptical as he was of the educational value of academic knowledge, both wanting and not wanting his children to secure academic degrees, feeling torn, possessing, despite his lack of formal education, an enormous appetite for the lyricism of Dante, Leopardi, Puccini. I could go on to link my family's proclivities to doubt our lovers and scrutinize our politics, religious faith, and one another to philosophical traditions that scrutinize the sanctities of faith and hope. And I could render scenes of teaching where skepticism seeped into my classroom, touching my curriculum entirely. But such a move, once again, would only serve as a defense against a more profound lesson my father handed down to me. From my father, I learned that knowledge and the body are often at war and, despite our apparent mastery of knowledge, our bodies too often remain vulnerable. In seeking knowledge, we are really seeking insight into what to do with our bodies, for teaching and scholarship are inevitably about decisions of the flesh.

In looking back, I learned to recognize that in the throes of illness, loss, or during a crisis in "meaning," there are cultural prohibitions placed on the expression of weakness, fear, and pain. But, perhaps more important, I have come to understand that the shameful, undisclosed suffering of the dead, suffering that could not be expressed, returns to their descendents and is unsuspected; this suffering continues to lead a painful half-life in them. Thus, the undisclosed suffering of my father, made manifest in his acute melancholia, lives on, haunting me in unsuspected ways, slipping into my pedagogy uninvited, compromising my capacity to refine my attachments to memory and history. From this point of view, a dividing line no longer falls between my father's life and death. His life and death can flow together, repeating and reinforcing each other *vis-à-vis* my teaching life.

In the narrative account I offer, I turn to teaching as a consolation for my loss, and this turn exacts a serious price. Not only do I position myself as a vulnerable daughter who inherits a scholarly and pedagogic project from her father, but, by using pedagogy as a consolation for loss, I displace my sense of abandonment, betrayal, and outrage rather than work through it.[13] My loss registers in strikingly apparent ways, for example, in the books that I choose to read with my students in courses I teach in curriculum studies, literacy, and English education. Among the books I choose are *Missing May* by Cynthia Rylant, *Krik? Krak!* by Edwidge Danticat, *My Brother* by Jamaica Kincaid, and *Fugitive Pieces* by Anne Michaels. Each of these stories portrays profound loss, from the death of a beloved aunt and a brother, to the horrific loss of life endured by the people of Haiti, to the brutalities of World War II. These books function like urns, holding loss, keeping it in place. As my students and I read *Krik? Krak!*, events that we have failed to learn about claim a presence in the room, a presence that leaves us speechless. Yet, to what extent do we use this book to console ourselves after learning of the U.S. involvement in Haiti and the horror of living under the brutal threats of the Tonton Macoutes? Do the routes that we take through Danticat's book only function to offer my students a narrative adjustment to loss, a consoling sign that enables each of us to adjust to the injustices that Danticat writes about? Do these consoling signs in turn distract us from properly remembering the dead? The historical figures in these stories are not easily quieted by the official discourses of monuments and memorials.

In her analysis of *Shot in the Heart,* the account by Mikal Gilmore of his family history and the execution of his brother, Gary, Leigh Gilmore emphasizes that "trauma causes history to erupt from its manageable confines. In this context, the dead are no longer persons who lived in the past, but angry, bitter, and mournful ghosts. The dead in this construction refuse to do the work of history, which is to stay buried, in effect, to 'be' the past, and to maintain the rationality of time as past-present-future. . . . The dead return because they were not properly buried" (2001, 5). To address trauma in the classroom raises questions, notes Gilmore, "about how the dead will permit and be permitted by the living to live on." Such questions invariably pose rhetorical challenges that are directly tied to melancholia, for melancholia is brought about by a "failed mourning," a failure that torments the melancholic by stealing speech because the losses that she has endured are not deemed grievable by our culture, and therefore they cannot be spoken aloud.

In *The Psychic Life of Power*, Judith Butler (1997) elaborates on the ways in which melancholia works as a lyric lament to protest our culture's narrow prohibitions on who can rightfully grieve, and which losses are worthy of attention. Following Butler, I want to argue that melancholy can be a rich resource for teaching and scholarship, for it holds nascent political texts that students and teachers can draw on to redraw the lines that demarcate their own psychic and social life, and, in turn, renegotiate the personal, social, and political prohibitions on grieving. The pedagogy of Anne Sexton offers us insight into how poetry and writing can be used to renegotiate these prohibitions, particularly the lecture notes she wrote while teaching at Colgate University during the spring term of 1972. These lecture notes provide a more complex way of putting melancholia to productive use in the classroom, offering us insight into the ways in which we might use poetry, performance, writing, and reading for learning about the transitions necessary to life, grieving being one among many of the vital transitions we can work through.

THE MELANCHOLIC PEDAGOGY OF ANNE SEXTON

Throughout Sexton's pedagogic documents are moments in which she directs her students' attention to social issues pertaining to the suffering, violated entity Elaine Scarry has termed "the body in pain."[14] The bodies in Sexton's poetry are most often women's bodies—one freshly scarred from a hysterectomy, a dying woman who is incontinent, a young girl giving up her baby, a daughter refusing to grieve—who speak to the reader through dramatic speech. When writing poetry with her students, Sexton asked them to use the force of dramatic consciousness to engage in composition processes that demanded what Sexton described as a "total immersion of you into the subject." In her poems, as she tells her students, we have the poet as actor:

> Wearing different faces; the young girl running from her lover ... the unknown girl giving her baby up so intensely, so close to the bone ... we have the seamstress bitter and gnarled over her sewing machine, spitting bile onto the zippers and we have the young lovers, the young girls specifically with her adulterous moment trying to marry for a moment at least some happiness.[15]

The acts of total immersion that Sexton engaged her students in often began with the invitation to "write a short poem, a character sketch using a persona ... become that person, put on that mask." The methods of dramatic introspection and incorporation that Sexton used to write poetry and to teach writing are strikingly akin to those used by actors as they work to build their characters. Nowhere are these methodologies more evident than in the notes she wrote for a course she taught as the Crawshaw Chair in Literature at Colgate University. The Crawshaw Chair required a long, weekly commute from Sexton's home in Weston, Massachusetts, to Hamilton, New York. Sexton was required to teach two days of classes back-to-back, a poetry writing workshop for about ten students in the evening as well as a lecture course on poetry in the afternoon. During the time Sexton commuted from Weston to Colgate, she often complained of feeling anxious to the point of nausea. Much of Sexton's teaching was accompanied by stage fright and uncertainty, and there were many bad days and fears of failure. Leverich describes Sexton as a shy, sensitive person who, on certain days, would sit at her desk in class, chain-smoking cigarettes, croaking out words between drinks of water. She seemed to him a desperately lonely creature. At the same time, there was a force, a charm, that was ever powerful about her. She was both bold and timid, dominant and passive, even impatient, yet understanding.

In a conversation I had with the chair of the Department of English at Colgate, Bruce Berlind recalled the difficult weekly routine of picking Sexton up at the airport in Syracuse, driving back to campus (frequently singing songs from the 1940s), and, the next day, driving back to the airport where she boarded a small plane for Boston. They co-taught the poetry workshop, and Sexton taught the lecture course alone. The lecture course, entitled "Anne on Anne," co-designed with Bruce Berlind, was composed of a series of eleven lectures for a small group of English majors. Berlind describes this course as a "course in herself":

> Its structure was simply linear, beginning with Bedlam and coming up-to-date. The lecture component of the classes was minimal. Mostly the classes were discussion sessions based on the students' readings of her books, copies of Anne's drafts of many poems, and copies of various interviews and reviews of her work. The "first-person presence" was, of course, at the center—although Anne often claimed that the *I* in poems dealing with her affairs was a fiction.[16]

According to Berlind, the aim of this course was to engage students imaginatively with the writing life of Anne Sexton by studying and then performing the interpretive methods she used to write poetry. Gathered together in Lawrence Hall, room 320, students would sometimes inhabit the poetic form of a Sexton poem and then extend it, at times changing the content, but miming the metrics. Sexton openly invited her students to study along with her what she referred to as the tricks, flaws, and false starts that a poem undergoes before it reaches its final, published form. Throughout her lecture notes are meditations on poetry, mini-lectures, and classroom assignments that suggest that Sexton was not satisfied with having her students talk about poetry. Rather, she demanded that they inhabit poetic forms and take on personae. In Lecture I of the Crawshaw series Sexton read the following statement by one of her critics: "Anne Sexton's poems, for example, create largely the world of her persona, the I of the poems, which undergoes a continuing development and is clearly related intimately and painfully to the poet's autobiography." She, in turn, responded to this statement by stating that

> I would like for a moment to disagree. It is true that I am an autobiographical poet most of the time, or at least so I lead my readers to believe. However,

many times I use the personal when I am applying a mask to my face, somewhat like a young man applying the face of an aging clown. Picture me at my
dressing table for a moment putting on the years. All those nights, all those
cups of coffee . . . all those shots of bourbon at 2 A.M. . . . all this applied like a
rubber mask that the robber wears.[17]

Like Sexton's composing processes, theories of melancholy evoke acts of
incorporation, skin, and the personal and cultural objects we endow with meaning. In ways akin to a method actor, the melancholic incorporates the dearly
beloved; she takes them in as idealized, demonized, in some cases, exoticized,
others. In his 1917 essay, "Mourning and Melancholia," Freud (1989) argues that
when a person has lost someone he or she loved, the ego incorporates aspects
of the lost other into its very structures, thereby "sustaining" the life of the
bereaved through acts of imitation. "By taking flight in the ego," writes Freud,
"love escapes annihilation" (630). Yet this escape from annihilation comes at
great cost, for the incorporative strategies used by the melancholic function to
disavow the loss and deepen the grief.

These incorporative strategies are an effective means through which to remake the ego into the person who has been lost. It is in this sense that the melancholic bears a resemblance to a method actor, for her body becomes a double
body, skilled at reproducing the gestures and being of some other person, a lost
love, a charismatic leader, the ethos of a nation.[18] The language that Constantin
Stanislavski used with his actors during rehearsals is replete with the language
of incorporation and is useful for understanding the strategies employed by the
melancholic. In *Building a Character*, Stanislavski (1945) documents a young
actor's discussion of the process he used to create the character of a man who
possessed distinctly different characteristics from himself. He writes:

. . . as soon as I was in this other man's skin, my attitude towards you [Stan-
islavski] underwent a radical change. . . . I enjoyed looking you full in the face
in a brazen way and at the same time felt I had the right to do it without fear.
Yet do you believe I could have done this in my own person? Never under any
circumstances! In that other person's skin I went as far as I liked, and if I dared
do that face to face with you I should have no compunction in treating the
audience across the footlights in the same way. (27–28)

The capacity to cross the boundaries of skin into the character of another,
and to do so with intention, caution, consistency, and to keep within the boundaries of the character, the play, or the "given circumstances," is work the actor,
unlike the melancholic, is adept at. The melancholic does not exert agency over
her desire to transpose the ego of the bereaved into her own. And while both
the actor and the melancholic may be skilled at transposition and incorporation, the actor retains these incorporative strategies as techniques, while for
the melancholic these strategies serve to chisel away at the ego, resulting in a
profound sense of ego loss.

Jacques Hassoun (1997) characterizes the melancholic as the eternally rav-
ished one, the passive victim, who is depleted of drives and thus incapable
of investing anything in the social world, sinking deeper and deeper into a
desperate, endless recitation of complaints that are directed at unnameable,
ungrievable losses. I find Hassoun's portrait of the melancholic only partly useful. In his analysis, he casts melancholia as a passive state wherein a person is
utterly stripped of agency and will. While this may in fact accurately capture
how some people experience loss after the death of a loved one, it does not fully
capture the attitude of revolt and feelings of anger that can also accompany the
melancholic. Returning to Freud, I found a somewhat different portrait, for
the plaints and endless lyric laments of the melancholic proceed, according to
Freud, from an attitude of revolt, a mental constellation by which the experience of loss has been transformed into melancholic contrition (1989, 169–170). I
want to proceed from the position of revolt and lyric lament that characterizes
much of Sexton's poetry to the place of her pedagogical performances. As I do
so, I want us to keep in mind that while the melancholic is overpowered, she
refuses to be tamed.[19]

Apparent Confessions

Sexton appeared to engage in self-conscious confessions in the seminar room,
displaying her own raw and visible wounds. Confessions work to enlist the
sororial and fraternal sympathies of the listener so as to exonerate the sinner
and, in turn, efface the differences between them. The confessional narrative
casts Sexton as the victim, and, through the medium of narrative, she passes
her guilt on to her students and readers. After all, we may very well summon
up some sympathy for Sexton, secretly finding that we are more like her than
we dared imagine, and, out of our own unexamined anxieties, we might very
well exonerate her.

Sexton openly admits to "doing reference work in sin," and to using her
place at the podium to seek "an appeal before a trial of angels." In one of her
lectures at Colgate, she brings her students back to the scenes that inspired her
poem "Flee on Your Donkey." She begins this lecture by telling her students
that they will learn things that "no one else in the world knows" from looking
at her worksheets. Back at the scenes that inspired this poem—a poem that
would take Sexton from June 1962 to June 1966 to complete—students learn of
Sexton's desire to flee not only from life but from madness. She confesses that
this is "a poem that everyone told me not to publish. It was too self-indulgent;
it was material I had already gone over. And yet, I hadn't told the full story of
my madness. I hadn't talked about fleeing it as well as fleeing life." Her lyric
laments persistently invoke the bodies of women who are confined, maimed,
dying, contemplating suicide, melancholic, medicated, or penetrated without
consent.

Yet, while Sexton appeared at every turn to confess her life repeatedly and unabashedly to her students, positioning herself as an apparent victim, her lyric laments and apparent confessions come from a mental constellation of revolt that is characteristic of melancholia. The term *melancholia* evokes more than depression or body chemistry gone awry. I do not wish to deny the biological dimension of melancholia. At the same time, however, it is important to recognize that melancholia contains the possibilities of articulating more fully the boundaries between psychic and social life, and, like every human emotion, it offers us the opportunity to gain insight into self and the Other. "Sadness," writes Michael Vincent Miller, "informs us that the loss was important; anger alerts us that the person in our path is an obstacle. Depression can be the most chastening state imaginable: it throws us back on our deepest sorrows and feelings of helplessness. What it may tell us about our limitations, our fears of abandonment, failure, death, ought not to be narrowed too quickly to a matter of neurotransmitters flowing between synapses" (qtd. in Hassoun, 1997, viii–ix).

The melancholic revolt expressed by Sexton is manifested both in the trope of the mask that appears throughout the Crawshaw lectures and in her parodic sensibilities. Sexton insisted on the fictive character of the *I* in her poems and explained to her students that, in the case of her poetry, "I am often being personal but I am not being personal about myself." Sexton's parodic sensibility functions to undermine the normative order of "performing confession" in the academy. Parody need not be comic. Derived from the Greek *parodia*, parody is a countersong, a neighboring song (Crapanzo, 1990, 144). Like melancholia, parody is structured in ambivalence, for it too has the paradoxical capacity both to incorporate and challenge that which it criticizes. There is a paradox inherent in the incorporative tactics of Sexton's composing processes: She simultaneously incorporates loss or lack in her body and disincorporates the authority of the master by wearing her wounds, or, to paraphrase Franz Fanon (1952), on the surface of her skin like an open sore—an eyesore to the colonizer.

The losses and ambivalence that Sexton carried into her teaching life manifest themselves, I believe, in a specifically performative approach to teaching writing. Put more directly, the performativity marking Sexton's teaching documents is drenched in melancholia, and these performances allegorize losses that are deemed ungrievable in academic institutions where grief is preempted by the absence of cultural conventions for avowing loss. I do not intend to suggest that all performative pedagogies are manifestations of trauma, but I do want to argue that there is social value in framing performative pedagogy as a structure of address that is directed toward loss. This value is articulated by Judith Butler: "Insofar as the grief remains unspeakable," writes Butler,

> The rage over the loss can redouble by virtue of remaining unavowed. And if that rage is publicly proscribed, the melancholic effects of such a proscription can achieve suicidal proportions. The emergence of collective institutions for grieving are thus crucial for survival, for reassembling community, for

rearticulating kinship, for reweaving sustaining relations. . . . What cannot be avowed as a constitutive identification for any given subject position runs the risk not only of becoming externalized in a degraded form, but repeatedly repudiated and subject to a policy of disavowal. (1997, 148–149)

By giving dramatic language to loss, Sexton demonstrates how pedagogy can be used to avow a broader range of subject positions in the classroom. Her use of performance accommodates the double-ghosted bodies that are housed in the melancholic. Performative modes of address have the capacity to bring about dialogue with the phantoms we hold, precisely because in performance the body is metonymic, of self, of characters, of voice, and of personae. As I said earlier, what marks the melancholic student is a loss of address, an unspeakability that is not a symptom of thoughtlessness or, what is often described in schools as "retrieval problems," but rather a symptom of what cannot be spoken in school. In my case, I failed to locate a narrative structure through which I could speak of and grieve my father's self-abuse and my sense of abandonment. Consequently, I used teaching as a means through which to compose a narrative that could contain my loss. This move, however, only served to harbor the not fully confronted phantoms or secrets from my earlier family history. The figure of Anne Sexton is but one example of an historical figure who I turned to in order to establish an addressable other through whom I could work through the losses that were encrypted in my pedagogy. In this sense, we might think of Anne Sexton as a mask through which I approached the secrets of my past, secrets that prevented me from using language in conventional or normative ways. Thus, the mask constitutes another kind of expressive contract; it organizes another operation of language.

The melancholic seeks an object that is continually out of reach, therefore posing a series of difficult challenges to writing and teaching: How do we teach a history that remains unnameable? How can we teach writing when the persons and objects one longs to make present are encrypted in a half-spoken history? Students who get lost in their own circuitous speech can often establish an object of address through the expressive registers of the mask and the persona. Because performance is contingent on physically establishing an addressable other—an audience—and crafting a character and a point of view (subjectivity), it offers a viable means through which to begin introducing the Other into pedagogy. In this sense, performative modes of address can ritualize melancholia by creating an occasion for writing that is open to the experience of inarticulateness and ambivalence that accompanies unnameable loss. Another important aspect of this approach to life writing includes the coordination of half-spoken personal loss with the larger historical field. This move to "conjugate" the personal with the social, theory, and history with literature opens texts up to meanings that have otherwise been foreclosed.

If I began this chapter in the archives in Austin, I want to end with a phone call to Aspen that was prompted by the love letter I found in the archives. On

February 18, 1998, I interviewed Chris Leverich. As far as he knows, Sexton never responded to his letter, although he did receive a B+ in the course. Leverich felt some satisfaction when I told him that Bruce Berlind vaguely recalls a remark made by Sexton suggesting that Leverich probably deserved an A because he was the only "really honest student in the class." During our conversation, Leverich remembered Sexton as fragile and sickly, suspicious, her eyes glazed over with tranquilizers. "I felt that she was working hard to get through the class. She was so terrified to be there, and you could see the terror in her body." When I asked Leverich what price he exacted as a student in her class, he told me that "Anne Sexton's teaching triggered for me a deep channel of emotion and areas of thought which were oftentimes frightening, so much so that I would push them aside. Sexton wrote and spoke to us about her deepest emotional and social involvements, and she taught me to address mine."

The exchanges among Anne Sexton, her students, and the personae in her poetry arguably offer a fresh representation of how the performative, "as if" position can be used to give shape to what students find difficult to articulate. Leverich's memories suggest that Sexton's pedagogy of masks presented her students with opportunities to approach, in some instances to wear, the masks of figures we find disquieting, excessive, or terrifying—figures who possess aspects of ourselves we have yet to confront and figures we have lost and loved. While the close reading of one student letter in the life of a teacher is not a sufficient basis from which to draw sweeping conclusions of either a theoretical or methodological nature, the act of interpreting the love letter Leverich substituted for Sexton's final assignment does provide an opportunity to reflect on specific questions concerning the generative force of half-spoken secrets associated with figures we long for, but who have passed on and left behind unresolved conflicts. In other words, Leverich's response to Sexton provokes us to think about the pedagogical uses of melancholia.

The love letter that Leverich substituted for Sexton's final assignment points to the ways in which, as teachers, we rarely know how our lessons are received or what lost loves, desires, or ideals they will summon up for our students. Grades do not present a meaningful picture of our teaching, nor do student evaluations or the solicited letters that sit in our tenure and promotion files. I suspect that Sexton unwittingly acted in ways that sustained Leverich's fantasies of her—sustaining in his imagination images of her as the ideal teacher, mother, sister, aunt, and, as he notes, father. At the outset of this chapter, I confessed to being worried about Sexton after I read this love letter. I worried that Leverich wanted to swallow his teacher up, to feed off of her, so to speak, having little conception of her as Other. To use his teacher well, the student must have a sense of boundedness, a sense that they are separate from one another and that an exchange is possible between them. As I noted earlier, Sexton never did respond to Leverich's letter, nor did she confer with him during the semester. According to Leverich, she really never noticed him at all. It's tempting for me to try to solve the riddle of this letter—to conclude this chapter by summing up what we can learn about pedagogy and melancholia before moving on. But if Sexton's pedagogical performances can teach us anything, it is the value of keeping our readings of her teaching life in play, not settling on which reading of her lectures is the true or most "knowing" one, which reading is right. The complex questions that melancholia raises for teaching—questions pertaining to loss like a loss of address, lost selves, ideals, and half-spoken secrets harbored by prior generations—point to the very educational value inherent in the *struggle* to articulate what our culture is ambivalent about or what our society and communities deem shameful. The melancholic cannot reproduce or prove the presence of the Object she longs for. One lesson offered to us by Anne Sexton, however, is that the melancholic can work at using the art of composing personae to restage the *effort* to remember her loss, thereby gaining insight into how loss can acquire meaning, and potentially generate recovery, not of the bereaved, but of herself, as the person who remembers.[20]

❧❧❧

As shown in the next chapter, which concerns the assignment that Leverich failed to hand in, the subject position that Sexton takes up is one of an 'unruly teacher,' whose academic taste is questionable. The final assignment, like the exercises she used in class, is performative in structure; it requires that students experiment with varying degrees of dramatic introspection, impersonation, and personae building. The narrative tactics that surface in the materials Sexton used while teaching at Colgate University unsettle the 'given' social expectations about the psychic, emotional, and physical borders that should circumscribe a teacher's body, particularly a female teacher who suffers with addictions and mental illness. Sexton's final assignment can be read as a parody of the expectations educators often harbor for their students—that they reproduce our ideas as well as the style and tastes we endow with meaning.

CHAPTER TWO

Teacher of "Weird Abundance"

A Portrait of the Pedagogical Tactics of Anne Sexton

Sexton is most often remembered as a "confessional" writer who, as Barbara Kevles wrote in 1976 (two years after Sexton's suicide), "jimmied open the family album to expose her suicide notes, filial guilt, madness, and longing for death. She would say the socially unacceptable things about herself that I never would" (1972, 47). Sexton had a knack for using commonplace minutiae such as pink slippers, a belly soft as pudding, a rolling pin, moss, blue stones, and bone to render scenes about the anguish of madness, early sexual distress, the shock of bereavement, the decay of Yankee families and houses. One critic wondered aloud if Sexton's messy preoccupations with adultery and incest and her heavily female and biological material will remain to stain the linen of the culture for long or whether good taste bleaches out even the most stubborn stains eventually (Ostriker, 1988, 263).

By many standards, Sexton was more rogue than fine artist, more trouble-maker than genteel poet. Alicia Ostriker admits

> that at her best she is coarse. Musically, Sexton's instrument is the kazoo. If Plath, say, is porcelain and Robert Lowell, bronze, Sexton is brightly colored earthenware. . . . She repeats herself without noticing. Her early poems before she hits her stride tend to be too stiff, her late ones tend to be shapeless. Her phrasing is sometimes sentimental, her endings sometimes flat. (1988, 265)

Literary taste was hard to come by for Sexton, particularly the taste valued in staid, genteel Boston. Sexton, who at one time sold cosmetics door-to-door and had but one year of college behind her, continually felt displaced in the academy. "I know that my academic background looks anemic and without much interest," she once wrote on an application for a fellowship, "but I have come a long way alone." Sexton's education was nonconventional in comparison to Sylvia Plath, Adrienne Rich, and her close friend and writing partner,

Maxine Kumin. While she continued her education at workshop tables led by Robert Lowell and W. D. Snodgrass at such prestigious institutes as the Antioch and Breadloaf Writer's, Sexton continually felt intellectually inadequate, a feeling that was only temporarily relieved by honorary doctoral degrees, a Bunting fellowship from Radcliffe, and book awards, including the Pulitzer Prize in 1967 for her third volume of poems, *Live or Die*. Sexton's feelings of displacement in the academy were further provoked by her critics, many of whom positioned her as a "primitive." A 1963 review of *All My Pretty Ones*, written by James Dickey, depicts those aspects of Sexton's poetry that readers found particularly distasteful. Directly assaulting her poetic approach, Dickey attacks her for "dwelling . . . insistently on the pathetic and disgusting aspects of bodily experience, as though this made the writing more real." He goes on to argue that

> it would also be difficult to find a more hopelessly mechanical approach to reporting these matters than the one she employs. . . . Her recourse to the studiedly off-hand diction favored by Randall Jarrell and Elizabeth Bishop and her habitual gravitation to the domestic and the "anti-poetic" seem to me as contrived and mannered as any poet's harking after galleons and sunsets and forbidden pleasures. (qtd. in Ostriker, 1988)

Dickey's review, like another written by Louis Simpson who criticized her poem, "Menstruation at Forty" as the "straw that broke the camel's back," haunted her and often provoked journalists such as Kevles to ask her, point blank, how she felt about such accusations. In a 1972 interview for the *Paris Review*, Kevles asks Sexton "if it is only male critics who balk at your use of the biological facts of womanhood." Sexton replied as follows:

> I haven't added up all the critics and put them on different teams. I haven't noticed the gender of the critic especially. I talk of the life-death cycle of the body. Women tell time by the body. . . . True, I get a little uptight when Norman Mailer writes that he screws woman anally. I like Allen Ginsberg very much and when he writes about the ugly vagina, I feel awful. That kind of thing doesn't appeal to me. So I have my limitations too. Homosexuality is all right with me. Sappho was beautiful. But when someone hates another person's body and somehow violates it, that's the kind of thing I mind. (190)

What Sexton suggests here is that the most distasteful of acts pivot not on portrayals of the body or the domestic but on violations of the body and an aggressive hatred of the female form. Not only do the bodies in Sexton's poetry depict crises and pain, but, as Sexton stands before her students, she, too, takes on the status of a grotesque figure whose body continually outgrew the socially sanctioned limits prescribed for women in the postwar era, limits that determined what it meant to be a respectable woman, mother, and teacher. Sexton was obscenely "off-balance," at times exuberant, at other times visibly suffering;

she was a teacher with a past, a figure of offense. Mary Russo (1994) describes the "grotesque body" in relation to the classical body, which is monumental, static, and closed. The grotesque body is democratically open and inclusive of the body at many stages of life—old age as well as youth, sickness as well as health. The grotesque images of the human body in Sexton's "confessions"—a body scarred from a hysterectomy or a dying woman who is incontinent—are multiple; they clamor, and are either bulging over or undersized, protuberant and incomplete. Sexton emphasizes the openings and orifices in these bodies, not their closure and finish. She gives the lower regions (legs, belly, feet, buttocks, genitals) priority over the upper regions (head, spirit, reason). The material bodies that take such a strong presence in Sexton's teaching documents can be interpreted as a form of what Bakhtin (1965) referred to as *grotesque materialism.* Grotesque materialism uses flesh conceptualized as corpulent excess to represent the social, topographical, and linguistic elements of the world. The grotesque realism infused in Sexton's pedagogy opposes a severance of the material body from conceptions of reason ascribed to the academic, the intellectual, or the "good" teacher. Moreover, the images of the grotesque body, like all body images, speak to us about social relations, social values, and collective identities (Stallybrass and White, 1986, 19).

The hatred of soft or abundant flesh or the "lower" bodily stratum is thinly veiled in the sarcastic tone that resonates in the reviews written by Dickey and Fein. *Sarcasm,* rooted in the Latin, "to cut flesh," is an effective rhetorical strategy for piercing the skin and hitting the bone. Apparently, the aim of these critics was not only to cut but also to cut deep.

And Sexton did feel cut again and again. Dickey had also reviewed her earlier work, *To Bedlam and Part Way Back,* claiming that she wrote like a student in a typical writing course. Humiliated, she told her psychiatrist, Dr. Orne, that "I lack taste, I haven't had the real foundation. . . . As a poet, it may be better to be crazy than to be educated. But I doubt it," she joked (Middlebrook, 1991, 126). Sexton tried to overcome what she saw as her educational disadvantage by enrolling in literature courses. Yet, during a summer course at Brandeis University in 1959, Sexton elected not to take the course for credit so that she would not have to take the exams. She could barely manage even a casual conversation with her instructors. "[Philip] Rahv asked me how I liked being a success . . . and I started to shake all over and couldn't even light a cig," she told W. D. Snodgrass (127–128).

Sexton protected herself from feeling pain by drinking, sometimes for days, before facing an audience. In a letter to Brother Dennis Farrell, a monk with whom Sexton corresponded between 1959 and 1962, she admitted

that the time I actually drink too much is when I go away as to give a reading at a college. Then I drink secretly in my hotel room for I am afraid to meet people, afraid of the audience, afraid of the deans and instructors etc. and determined to impress them. . . . At Cornell, I was there five days during a great conference. . . . In five days I could hardly sleep and my engine went only on booze. When I got home I slept for 52 hours straight. I must learn moderation in all things, my Dr. tells me. You see, I am given to excess. That's all there is to it. I have found that I can control it best in a poem . . . if the poem is good then it will have the excess under control . . . it is the core of the poem . . . there like stunted fruit . . . unseen but actual. (L. Sexton and Ames, 1977, 143–144)

The numbing effects of alcohol would eventually dim Sexton's poetic sensibilities. By late 1973, Sexton had begun to drink around the clock, from rising to sleeping. As Sexton approached the end of her life, she became more shrill, more outrageous, and more demanding, carrying small vials of vodka with her everywhere. "Even," recalls her daughter, Linda Gray Sexton, "to faculty meetings at Boston University, where she passed them under the table to her colleague, John Cheever" (L. Sexton, 1994, 169). Yet, during the last years of her life, when her alcoholism and mental anguish were most severe, Sexton managed to continue working at Boston University, where she taught until her suicide on Friday October 4, 1974.

The figure of Anne Sexton constitutes the site not only of an unruly woman who is perceived as lacking academic taste but of one who embodies the despised and feared aspects of female subjectivity—madness, anxiety, and an unruly body that cannot be contained, cured, or consoled by normative prescriptions. At issue is the question of what affects Sexton's taste for the grotesque exerted in the seminar room. To what extent does Sexton's deployment of grotesque materialism, with all its accompanying marks of excess that threaten to outgrow and seep through standardized limitations, offer us cues for using parody, exaggerations, and inversions to decenter our own pedagogical performances? What might the assignments that Sexton designed for her students tell us about the construction of the female subject in education, particularly a subject who is drawn to performative modes of address—that is, to a mode of address that is contingent on a form of "acting out," and articulating loss?

To work through these questions, I perform a series of readings of the final assignment that Sexton developed for her students at Colgate University. The performative features of this assignment, like the overall course design of "Anne on Anne," invite students to experiment with varying degrees of dramatic introspection and personae building. These conventions are used, once again, to direct her students' attention to her poetry where they encountered the suffering, violated and often grotesque images of bodies in pain.[1] In much of Sexton's poetry, she maps out the geography of the madhouse, psychic disequilibrium, and the sociality of women who are "tired of the spoons and the pots . . . the cosmetics and the silks . . . tired of the gender of things" (1988a, 83). To "confess" about matters pertaining to the lower bodily stratum, the underworld of madness, emotional instability, or unconventional desires is to transgress the rules of hierarchy in four symbolic domains: the psychic, the domain of the human body, geographical space, and the social order. "Cultures think themselves," write Peter Stallybrass and Allon White, "in the most immediate and affective ways through the combined symbolisms of these four hierarchies ... transgressing the rules of hierarchy and order in anyone of the domains may have major consequences in the others" (1986, 3). And while Sexton's use of dramatic conventions such as impersonation and masks did indeed function to transgress the rules of hierarchy in these four domains outlined above, her acts of transgression also exacted a serious price. The association of women with performance and masquerade perpetuates demeaning representations (and in the case of Sexton, misogynistic) representations of female subjectivity. Thus, we need to approach her pedagogy with this in mind.

In the following pages, I thematize some of the tactical maneuvers. Sexton used to transgress the psychic domain and the domain of the human body while teaching poetry at Colgate University.[1] Embedded in the notes that Sexton prepared for her courses at Colgate is a constellation of negotiations with the classic academic culture based on what Michel de Certeau calls the "tactics" of people who are subordinated and weak and who have no space of their own. To identify the space needed to make up a series of tactical maneuvers, de Certeau distinguishes between a tactic and a strategy. Strategies are legitimate ways of doing things. They constitute a readily identified system of operations in which the borders between the strategy and that which it operates on are clear and distinct. One example of such a strategy is Immanuel Kant's approach to discriminating between aesthetic and sensory pleasure. Kant bestowed great social importance on the aesthetic, while relegating the sensory to the level of the low and the base. To establish a true aesthetic experience requires a level of reflection on the object, which is what distinguishes it from the lowly sensory encounter. This visual appreciation, or way of looking, works as a "strategy" through which to understand a "nature" or object that is perceived as distinct from the rules and procedures that constitute it.

The opportunities to make up and practice tactics, on the other hand, emerge in our daily life and are mixed up with sensation and reflection, looking and feeling—eating, shopping, reading, cooking, and so on. Tactics are "fragmentary and fragile;" they are "seized on the wing," clever tricks, knowing how to get away with things, polymorphic simulations, joyful discoveries, poetic as well as warlike. "The space of the tactic," writes de Certeau, "is the space of the other," for the weak do not have a space of their own; their terrain is "organized by the law of a foreign power." Recognizing that what the weak win they cannot keep, he argues that they appropriate spaces of the dominant culture for their own uses—or make them "habitable, like a rented apartment ... transform another person's property into a space borrowed for a moment" (de Certeau, 1984, xix, xxi, 25, 37). Because it does not have a place, a tactic depends on timing and repartee. "This temporal category belongs to the improvisational, to the realm of what is possible, not in the future, but in very specific historical moments," and for very specific and practical purposes.[2] These possibilities are composed through meticulous attention paid to the circumstances at hand.

The narrative tactics that surface in Sexton's teaching materials unsettle the "given" social expectations and anxieties about the psychic, emotional, and physical borders that should circumscribe a teacher's body. Rather than being poised as a female teacher who represents elevated forms of culture, Sexton represents the actual lived-in female body in post–World War II America, providing us with a metonymic reminder of sexual difference and the contingencies between middle-class life and madness, anxiety and teaching, sickness and health. Housed in Sexton's addicted and anxious body are the symptoms of a woman who must keep secrets, secrets about her body as a site of abuse and a site of loss, and perhaps most relevant to pedagogy are symptoms that are tied to feelings of profound displacement, in the academy, at home, and among her family. Sexton's pedagogical tactics constitute a "logic of action" for the displaced who must learn to transform "another person's property into a space borrowed for a moment by a transient" (de Certeau, 1984, xxi). Sexton, as pedagogue, appears to know intimately about the subtle art of "renters" who are knowledgeable about how to insinuate their countless differences into the dominant texts of the academy (xxii).

The final assignment that Anne Sexton presented to her students on the first day of class at Colgate is literally an invitation to impersonate her, to play off the/her academic body by taking on the multiple perspectives of the grotesque characters in her poems. This act of impersonation also subverts the rhetoric of warfare so replete in academia, transforming a *mise-a-mort* into a more ludic form of experimentation and play. Finally, Sexton's pedagogical tactics also place the limitations of de Certeau's concepts in relief, for de Certeau's use of warfare imagery and his tendency to romanticize the difficult labor of inventing tactics in everyday life at times positions the tactician as an exotic, abjected "Other," thereby perpetuating a conservative history of domination.

"YOU ARE TO FABRICATE MY REPLY . . ."

As a final assignment for the course "Anne on Anne," students were to write an interview in which they fabricated a persona from the details in Sexton's poems and lectures. In preparation for this final project, students were asked to read the various critiques of her work as well as her five books. Additionally, they were asked to bring questions to class each week for Sexton to answer. "But not until you have already given your answer," Sexton informed them on the first day of class. "In other words," continues Sexton,

> you are to fabricate my reply and we will see how close you come as the term moves on. In the beginning a question a week will do and we'll see how that goes. However, by May 3rd, the next to the last class, I would like a completed interview, cohesive, integrated, thematic, handed in. About a fifth of it should be fresh material that has never been done in class or done just that way. You may take note of other people's questions and use them if they seem to fit into

your piece. You might take one aspect and go into depth. When you hand in these questions weekly, I would like them typed just as, of course, the final interview will be typed.... For the first eight classes, there will be in-class assignments. Written work that will let you live the life of a poet. I realize you are not all writers, but you will know a lot more about writing and the way a writer thinks after doing them. And thus will know me better. Some of these will be read aloud in class. Along with all this I will give my mini-lectures and we will pick apart and analyze and discover together sixty-eight of my poems. We will look at the worksheets of three and discover together my tricks and flaws.[3]

She concludes this description by assuring her students that they will look at the interviews written about her together. "I will read one of them to you today to give you a feeling of how it can be done. Both this and the *Paris Review* interview ought to be in the library for you to look at."[4]

As I first read through this assignment, I felt overwhelmed by the excessive accumulation of personae—fabricate a persona from Sexton's poems, formulate a question a week for Sexton, formulate an answer, see how close you come to her response as the term moves on? What, I imagined myself asking Sexton, is really going on here? And why an interview? Was Sexton playing off the *Paris Review* interview with Barbara Kevles in which she was inadvertently asked to defend herself against claims that she was a "primitive"? To what extent did Sexton ask her students to deploy the genre of the interview from a position of debasement?

Perhaps Sexton unwittingly asked her students to "act out of character" so that they could parody the formal narrative logic which ordinarily structures the college English assignment, a logic whereby the act of incorporating the teacher is mandatory but rarely, if ever, mentioned. Acts of incorporation constitute a complex and vital means through which we learn, fraught as they are with anxieties about what we desire and what we loathe, who we want to be, who we fear, and what we work hard to forsake. By asking her students to approach and then incorporate pieces of her "grotesque" body, and to incorporate aspects of a composing process that contains striking elements of a grotesque materialism, Sexton raises important questions, not only about the ways in which our students imbibe, through spoken and unspoken exchanges, formal and informal, our culture's body habits, language systems, memories, values and anxieties, but also how we determine what is normal and what is perverse, what will come in and what we will spit out. When I ask educators to read this assignment they are often put off, at times outraged by the apparently narcissistic features of Sexton's requirements. Some teachers argue that this assignment masquerades as a lure through which to trap students into doing nothing short of learning to recognize themselves in Sexton's image, for clearly a student's success in this class was contingent upon how proficient they became at impersonating the composing processes of Anne Sexton—coming closer throughout the term to thinking like her, to virtually becoming her.

Such requirements run counter to our conscious beliefs in liberatory pedagogies that are committed to providing spaces for students to bring their histories, beliefs, and values to bear on the curriculum, working, as it were, toward
negotiating an enlarged awareness of and perspectives on the personal in the
political and the ways in which the recesses of the personal hold history's most
intricate and evaded invasions.[5] The expressed anxieties about this assignment,
many of which I also shared, point, I believe, to our reluctance to consider the
extent to which we, too, may be complicit in composing a curriculum that
is tainted by our own narcissistic attachments. This assignment is grotesque
precisely because it dramatically exaggerates and brings to the surface aspects
of our pedagogy that we prefer to remain silent or hidden, provoking us to
consider the extent to which we ask our students to become the intellectual
companions we long for. Perhaps we are more like Sexton than we dare imagine, and it is in this sense that Sexton provokes educators to take seriously the
question of taste, asking that we address the specific practices through which we
lure students into adapting our tastes and incorporating the bodies of literature
that we endow with meaning.

Both taste and incorporation invoke images of the mouth and the craving
for other mouths—in a word, kissing—which, as Adam Phillips (1996) reminds
us, is

> an act in which we devour the object by caressing it; we eat it, in a sense, but
> sustain its presence. Kissing on the mouth can have a mutuality that blurs the
> distinctions between giving and taking ("In kissing do you render or receive,"
> Cressida asks in Troilus and Cressida).... Kissing though, is the sign of ...
> controlling the potential—at least in fantasy—to bite up and ingest the other
> person. Lips as it were, are the next thing to teeth, and teeth are great educa-
> tors. (96–97)

The fantasy that our students will incorporate us lingers around the edges of
theories of language learning, suggesting that students need opportunities not
simply to imitate us but to take the knowledge we offer them into their bodies, while we strive to sustain rather than devour their presence. In this sense,
teaching and learning, at their best, are a bit like kissing, for the kiss offers us
an image of reciprocity, not domination. Like teaching, kisses can be highly
stylized and formal, canonic if you will. Kisses can also be fused with the shock
of newness that brings with it all the excitement, anxiety, and uncertainty we associate with our first days of teaching, or the first day of class, or when we teach
something that we have never taught before. There are terrifying kisses that
make us feel strange, occupied, just as there are terrifying teachers who make us
feel as if we were being swallowed up, disappearing in their gaze. And there is
the kiss that is so suffused with emotion that we hold it in the sinews beneath
our skin, for with this kiss we do not feel abandoned, or devoured; rather we
feel the vibrancy, weight, and radiance—even if for a moment—of our own
presence in the presence of another. Kissing, like teaching and learning, involves

us in the highly charged and sometimes, in the words of Phillips, "dangerous allure and confusion of mistaken identity, of getting muddled up" (1996, 100). In the context of the classroom, who we are to one another often gets confusing. Teaching and learning are themselves occasions for getting muddled up, and the work of incorporation is wrought with unanticipated invitations for doing so, invitations that we rarely speak of, invitations that can be eerily uncanny. Who was Sexton to her students and who was she to them as they took up a process of coming to know, in her words, "a lot more about writing and the way a writer thinks"?

In her study of pedagogy and object-relations theory, Wendy Atwell-Vasey (1998) draws extensively on the work of Julia Kristeva to illustrate that learning is not solely a mimetic process, but rather is contingent on complex processes of incorporation and abjection. Incorporation finds students tracing the patterns that are enacted by the teacher, a performative process that Julia Kristeva (1989) refers to as reduplication. Reduplication offers us a more generative way to think about incorporation precisely because reduplication does not presume a ready-made, fully composed ego in relation to an already composed object.[6] Nor does the process of reduplication suggest images of devouring and subsuming subjects. Atwell-Vasey further renders the qualities of incorporation by underscoring its performative features, emphasizing that students do not know a set of pragmatic codes, for example, as things in themselves, but rather, through acts of incorporation, they come to know the function, the place, the feel, and the pulse that such things take on in their lives.

By rereading Sexton's final assignment as a form of incorporation of a particular sort, that is, a form of incorporation that is in effect a reduplicating process, we can more fully apprehend what Sexton sought to accomplish through that assignment, for she asks students not simply to imitate her but to incorporate her by tracing the patterns of her thoughts and uses of language, rhythm, and meter, to reduplicate them, and to locate the function that these patterns might take on in their own lives. In tracing the patterns of her thoughts and her poetry and in treating her work as continuously open and in motion, she potentially creates spaces for students to explore the outposts of their unstable or forsaken identities.[7]

The process of reduplication is evident in a number of the questions that Sexton posed to her students, questions that stress that they become involved with her poetry by walking a fine line between becoming a part of her and not a part. Her questions ask them to reflect their readings back to her as an addressee, but at the same time to infuse their responses with their own sensibilities and experiences. "What is the best line in the poem? Describe one of the personae in these poems as if you had just met them, or were observing them. . . . Your assignment in class for this week is another either/or. Write a short character study of the interrogator of 'The Man of Many Hearts' or write more questions that he might have asked. See if you can expand his voice."[8] As students shift over to the place of the poet by exploring her work and then thread their subjectivities through this work—"You will bring questions to class each week for me to answer. But not until you have already given your answer"—they reduplicate her composing processes by "performing the functions she performs" so as to remake their subjectivities through the prism of the composing processes, poetry, and critiques of Anne Sexton.

These spaces, however, contain uncanny figures, illness, and the threat of loss through disease and mental anguish. In addition, the "functions" she performs are contingent on coming in close to rather than taking a view from a cold and calculated distance. Coming in close to disease and anguish, particularly in the presence of a teacher who suffers from alcoholism, anxiety and visible despair, imposes a certain horror in the classroom. As parents and teachers, we often assume that the classroom will hide, in its forgotten margins, all the horrors that are felt in the wake of death and illness, fears and phobias. What is at stake when these emotions return with intensity to haunt the imaginations of those who have struggled to render spaces to protect their health and their happiness? The case of Anne Sexton poses difficult questions about how to negotiate a respectful distance between teacher and student, student and text, when the spaces of exile, asylum, confinement, quarantine, and senility continuously spill into the "normal" space of the seminar room, blurring the boundaries between the organic space of the teacher's body and the social space in which that body lives and works, domains we can no longer identify as separate but that continue to be surveyed by transparent forms of power.[9]

Sexton was admittedly unskilled at negotiating the proper distance between her and others. In her memoir, *Searching for Mercy Street: My Journey Back to My Mother*, Linda Gray Sexton writes about the shame and terror that was attached to living with a mother who knew little about the limits between her body and her daughter's. On one level, Sexton's strongest influence as a mother was defined by her repeated absences while she was hospitalized. On another level, her influence was defined by an inability to establish and sustain limits between herself and others. "Mother had never had good control over herself," writes Linda.

> Her inability to set limits for herself, to refrain from acting out nearly every impulse, often led us into difficult, traumatic situations. Thus, it is not surprising that her psychological intimacy with me on the subject of sexual matters, her pressure for me to have sex and then report back on it, her curiosity about my body and the ways it was changing as I moved into adolescence, were mirrored by a disturbing physical intimacy. (1994, 106)

Sexton intruded on Linda's sexual life in unimaginable ways, leaving her feeling ashamed and surveyed. As I reread the final assignment that Sexton announced to her students on the first day of class, I detected traces of Sexton's proclivity to act out, to introduce unspeakable subjects—in a word, to come in too close.[10]

And then I began to feel the psychic boundaries between myself and Sexton blur; I felt the tug of a lure, a strange mix of desire and anxiety, as I began to imagine how this hot mix of emotions would surge through my body had I actually been sitting in Lawrence Hall. If I were to play at being Sexton, then who would I be in this class, what would become of my identity as a student, particularly as a female attending this until recently all-male institution? At this moment I felt incapable of capturing the significance of this assignment. At the same time, I could not come to a halt and stop at the surface of it and move on to something else. I felt arrested in a state of anxiety.

"The field of anxiety," argued Lacan (1962), "is framed by the uncanny, as the uncanny itself is framed as a sudden apparition seen, as it were, through a window, a skylight, a keyhole." The feeling of suddenness, of the "all at once," is crucial for Lacan in setting the scene of uncanny anxiety, and it is this scene that came to mind as I imagined myself sitting in Sexton's class, wading through the parameters of this assignment. Lacan likens a feel for the uncanny to the sensation we feel immediately before the curtain goes up in the theatre, provoking the audience to prepare for a "state of alert." But the crucial feature of the uncanny that is of most relevance to my study of Anne Sexton is the fact that the uncanny provokes anxiety because something appears that was already there, something closer to the house, the heim: the host. What suddenly appears at the door of the home, or on the stage, is at once hostile and expected, foreign to and yet embedded in the house. This dangerous conjunction, teacher + addict, teacher + mental illness, transformed the archive into a panic space where all the traditional limits I had clung to as I began to render her teaching life became blurred. I kept returning to what sounded like a refrain to me, at times, a challenge: "And we will see how close you come as the term moves on."

What truths are told by my anxious response to this assignment? The kind of truth I am invoking here is an ideal urged by Andrea Dworkin, Jose Zuniga, Adrienne Rich, and most recently David Bleich. To speak the truth means to speak in public, "to achieve" writes Bleich,

> an ability to discern how our language tells the truths of history and experience in our lives as they affect our involvement in a subject matter. . . . If these meanings also alert us to previously unexamined actions of academic, athletic, military, or domestic memberships, we have perhaps told more of the truth about how our subject matter contributes to society. (1998, 112)

Dworkin urges writers to "reclaim the language from those who use it to justify murder, plunder, violation" (1974, 24–25).

There were so many components to this assignment that made me uneasy: flesh, mirrors, lyricism, performativity. In a word, all these aspects made me worry about a curriculum that might fall too heavily on the side of the soft, contradicting the traces of a masculine pedagogy that I had so dutifully inherited. To what extent, I wondered, did this assignment leave spaces for anything but fusion and merging?

The masculine project that was apparently absent in Sexton's seminar room uses speech genres in agonistic, competitive ways, a rhetorical tradition Walter

Ong identifies with the channeling of aggression into accepted cultural forms, much like Freud's sanctioned process of channeling grief into forms of cultural work.[11] Ong (1981) associates this tradition with male subjectivity, specifically because men traditionally controlled literacy and public forms of culture. The word *ludus*, writes Ong, was Latin for both game and school, and originally referred to a preparation for war. The narrative contest is a highly developed cultural game, a game that involves, in the same way as an academic debate, a symbolic execution, a verbal *mise-a-mort* (see Ong, 2002). In narrative, as in rhetoric or analytic philosophy, texts are indeed the weapons in the fight for life, but in Sexton's pedagogy she used writing to save her own life, and this fight was not fused with an agonistic competitive spirit or the intent to wipe out an enemy. Rather it revolved around relating and textualizing encrypted memories, a process that both used and sought to break through the rules of standardized representation.

The lyric structure that Sexton uses in this assignment invites her students to do what we do in lyric poetry: rather than remaining outside the representational frame and judging it, we imaginatively participate in the character's localized, immediate situation, being drawn most directly to the emotional life in the scene. The double-bodied presence that Sexton's assignment is contingent on—I must play both myself and Sexton, both Sexton and a persona in her poems—puts her students in close proximity to the grotesque bodies that she invokes as a teacher and a writer.[12] These doubled bodies, with all their potential for excess, produce further possibilities for the kinds of replications, divisions, and multiple formations that Freud identifies in his discussion of the double in relation to the notion of the unheimlich, or uncanny. The redoubled and ghostly body lives at the site of the maternal, threatening to reproduce monstrously: "In other words," writes Freud, "there is a doubling, dividing and interchanging of the self. And finally there is the constant recurrence of the same thing—the repetition of the same features of character traits or vicissitudes, of the same crimes, even the same names through several consecutive generations" (Freud, 1919, 233–238). What could possibly come of this assignment that could be remotely worthwhile? What pedagogical crimes did I fear were being committed here?

To be frank, I feared that Sexton had no place in the classroom. Yet, at the same time, the testimony I had been reading over the years made me conclude something else—that she was indeed a diligent and devoted teacher. As I looked closer at this assignment, I detected specific ruptures in the lure to merge into one, producing the potential for a contingent rather than continuous relationship with the figure of the teacher/poet. Freud posits that the double, that is, a person's capacity to treat a remaining part of the ego as an object, to reflect on it so to speak, holds "all the unfulfilled but possible futures to which we still like to cling in phantasy, all the strivings of the ego which adverse circumstances have crushed, and all our suppressed acts of volition which nourish us in the illusion of Free Will" (Phillips, 1996, 31). Thus, the presence of the uncanny double feels nostalgic not only for the past but for possible futures as well, where a person is drawn to those aspects of life that various commitments have left out of the picture. I found myself questioning the extent to which Sexton may have used her pedagogical tactics as forms of reparation through which to establish the "proper" distance between herself and others, a distance that was not keyed to standard codes but allowed room for her students to read and write her life without feeling surveyed and dangerously vulnerable in the ways that her own two daughters often had. Did genres such as the lyric and the elegy, the play and the interview, provide Sexton with a repertoire of "potential spaces" she could offer her students, a repertoire that was not composed of imitations of canonical texts but rather an improvisation off them, a reduplicating process that brought her students closer to articulating themselves with respect to her work? And did this potential space also offer her students a means through which to address her life and she theirs without slipping into empathic states that worked solely to devour rather than to incorporate one another?

A WALK IN THE CITY

The call for impersonation and the images of double bodies generated by this assignment raise important questions about the promise and the trouble of using masquerade and other dramatic conventions as pedagogical tactics. To consider more closely the promise, let us look to de Certeau, for the lyric feel to Sexton's assignment invokes his trope of a "walk in the city," in his case Manhattan, where we begin by viewing this urban landscape from the 110th floor of the World Trade Center, reading this "giant rhetoric of excess in both expenditure and production" from a great distance, in general and gross terms. In de Certeau's words:

> When one goes up there, he leaves behind the mass that carries off and mixes up in itself any identity of authors or spectators. An Icarus flying above these waters, he can ignore the devices of Daedalus in mobile and endless labyrinths far below. His elevation transfigures him into a voyeur. It puts him at a distance. It transforms the bewitching world by which one was "possessed" into a text that lies before one's eyes. It allows one to read it, to be a solar Eye.... The exaltation of a scopic and gnostic drive: the fiction of knowledge is related to this lust to be a viewpoint and nothing more ... the totalizing eye imagined by the painters of earlier times live on in our achievements. (1984, 92)

De Certeau urges us to make our way down from the 110th floor, and take to walking in the streets below, "below thresholds at which visibility begins" (1984, 93). This move constitutes a lyric shift from panoptic power. Sexton, too, is asking her students to be walkers, to follow the thicks and thickets of her grotesque texts, to come up close, at times stand face to face with the figures in her poetry, and to enter places such as the madhouse, where Anne, as a persona "chews in rows and stands in broken lines," walking through "the antiseptic tunnel" in this "summer hotel with the plastic sky, the best ward in bedlam." In asking her students to take on persona and to "fabricate her reply," to interview her and develop questions of their own design, Sexton works to intervene in the scopic drive, the lust to view a poetic text and a poet's body from a cold distance, to totalize and possess its meaning. Rather than taking the well-trodden path of formal analysis, whereby the students hold her poetry and her person at a distance, Sexton proposes that they invent a collaborative subject "Anne Sexton." Perhaps Sexton longs for her students to rewrite a local narrative of her biography, life, and art, one that does not reduce her to categories and easy cliches. Walking offers us opportunities for a series of turns and detours, which can be compared to "turns of phrase" or "stylistic figures" that require style and art. The physical, visceral rhetorical forms that de Certeau renders make a case for the use of the lyric and improvisational moves that Sexton draws on in her classes, positing them as pedagogical tactics for symbolically inverting the political game that students are implicitly asked to engage in—not only to imagine or guess (excessively) at what the teacher wants but to give the teacher what she wants.

On the other hand, however, Sexton's use of impersonation filled me with ambivalence. Her pedagogic tactics are loaded with all the connotations of fear and loathing that surface in the presence of the essentialized image of the polymorphous shape of the female body. This body without a beginning and an end, which parallels the hysterical crisis, potentially endangers itself by equating the female form with madness and death.[13] The unbounded body of the hysteric is locked in the attic, the house, or the asylum where she can be looked at, stared at, but not understood. The gestures and pain of the grotesque figures invoked by Sexton, while defiant, are in danger of putting themselves out of circulation, "seen but not heard" (Russo, 1994, 68).

Sexton's excessive, hyperbolic pedagogy, her "overacting," can be read as a performance doubled over with meaning wherein she mimics the classic pedagogic relationship between teacher and student, again asking students not only to guess at what the teacher wants but to give excessively the teacher what she wants, and of course, to incorporate her. Luce Irigary (1985) describes this mimetic tactic as a means through which to "make visible" by an effect of playful (and I would add lyric and localized) repetition what was supposed to remain invisible: the cover-up of the mimetic effects of our pedagogical demands. Or, to put it another way, the cover-up of our own desires to position our students as recognizable others, as subjects of difference that are almost the same as us, but not quite. By using the phrase "almost the same, but not quite," I intend to point to the sense of ambivalence I experienced as I initially read this assignment—again, how close should Sexton's students come to her academic body, what aspects of her composing process should her students take in, what anxieties and language systems should they spit out? The ambivalences generated by Sexton's final assignment produce slippages, excess, and high degrees of indeterminacy. In instructing her students to "fabricate her reply," she effectively composes an assignment that both resembles and is a menace to many of the assignments we design for our students, thereby problematizing, at times parodying, what we take to be normative pedagogical practice. The menace of mimicry lies precisely in its double vision, which in disclosing its ambivalence with respect to dominating discourses also disrupts its authority, uttering what is known and must be kept concealed; a discourse described by Homi Bhaba that is uttered between the lines and as such speaks both against the rules and within them (1994, 89).

✻✻✻

The acts of incorporation suggested by Sexton's pedagogy engage students in taking up the tastes of others, particularly "outlawed" others, figures who have spent time in the madhouse, the woman whose fears confine her to her home, women who are grieving, dying and lost. The double-bodied consciousness called for in the final assignment functions as a pedagogical practice that exemplifies what it might mean for students to play through fictive scenarios, performing the tastes of others as "styles of the flesh," each of which, writes Judith Butler, "have a history which conditions and limits possibilities, each of which is both intentional and performative, where 'per formative' suggests a dramatic, contingent, and imaginative construction of meaning" (1990, 139).

Indeed, Sexton's pedagogical performances might be read as characterizations of a teacher perpetually in "error." Unlike the pedagogical models that are allied to progress, rationality, and liberation and that disassociate themselves from their mistakes and their anxieties, Sexton's "grotesque performances" place her at risk for being perceived as a "demon" and a "primitive." At the same time, she devised effective pedagogical tactics for avowing the troubled body in the writing classroom. Her pedagogical tactics drew on classic poetic and rhetorical forms, protocols and styles of canonic culture, but did so from the position of debasement. Sexton mobilized masks to resist, exaggerate and destabilize the distinctions and strict boundaries that mark and maintain positions of privilege in the academy and, by doing so, she exceeded perceptions of what constitutes "academic work" in the writing classroom.

Like the stunts of tightrope walkers and aerialists that Mary Russo so astutely turns to for instruction, Sexton's pedagogy required excellent timing, discipline, determination, skill and stamina. The figure of Sexton as teacher is represented in the double meaning of the word *stunt*, for Sexton embodies both an image of female exceptionalism as well as that of a dwarfed creature in the pedagogical sideshow whose (disciplinary) body is monstrous and lacking in height, esteem, and taste (Russo, 1994). The critiques waged against Sexton, like many of the concerns expressed over personal writing today, hold a fear that affairs of the body, particularly the body of females, will contaminate academic work and classroom discourse. As a limit case in teacher education, Sexton portrays forms of imaginative resistance to an academic body that are immortalized in the academy, an esteemed body that speaks a lean, fit discourse, and never indulges in the excess that impersonation demands. Sexton's pedagogy cues educators to develop more refined tastes for irony, parody and the grotesque so that we might redefine the limited tastes that represent "rationality" and emotional reliability in our classrooms. Not, however, by linking the grotesque with the grotto-esque cave and then moving rapidly to the womb of woman-as-mother, leading us toward a regressive, psychic register.

Rather, as Sexton's grotesque figures move, they presuppose that our bodies are in process; they both grow and decay, accumulate mastery and endure vulnerability. In this sense, the uncanny figures of the grotesque in Sexton's work gesture continually toward the potential for self-invention and reinvention, seeking varied ways to live, teach, and learn in the face of material, psychic, and political limitations, offering educators a possible means through which to remap the terrain of subjectivity so as to keep alive and possible myriad ways of be-longings, desired, virtual, respectful connections to one another, refusing the easy fix, the static and extremes of either a classic or grotto-esque pedagogy. Read in this light, the pedagogical tactics of Anne Sexton suggest possible ways for educators to compose spaces for learning and teaching that are unassimilable to the normal, controlled, anaesthetized spaces that create binary divisions—public and private, past and present, the psyche and the social—urging us to work toward developing an interstitial intimacy.

CHAPTER THREE

Something Worth Learning

A Reading of the Student-Teacher Relationship
Between Anne Sexton and John Holmes

The difference between mad people and sane people . . . is that sane people
have variety when they talk story. Mad people have only one story that they
talk over and over. . . .

—*Maxine Hong Kingston, in* Woman Warrior

On Monday, January 30, 1961, Anne Sexton sent a letter to John Holmes. Her
letter was a response to accusations Holmes made that she had acted selfishly
and without sensitivity at a poetry workshop a few weeks earlier. Most hurtful,
however, was the anger he expressed at Sexton for making a spectacle of herself—not only during the weekly poetry workshops they conducted with poets
Maxine Kumin and George Starbuck, but in her poetry as well.

> It has taken me this many days to get over your letter—that is, this many days
> to love you again and this many days to love me again. For one, I'm not going
> to beat around the bush. Your letter hurt me. More than you could imagine. . . .
> Can't you perhaps help me with the real problem instead of just telling me that
> I am rather selfish and then in turn thoughtless and then, what's worse, very
> cruel. I may be noisy—but I'm not cruel and I never have been. (L. Sexton
> and Ames, 1977, 117, 119)

John Holmes was Sexton's first poetry teacher, but he was not the first
person to accuse Sexton of getting too close to that specifically feminine
danger of exposure—of losing boundaries, and of failing to be attentive
enough to the reserved timing and formal repartee that he valued at the workshop table. Like many of her critics, Holmes criticized Sexton for failing to

distance herself from the emotional material in her poetry. He believed that she brought her readers "too close to home" by offering them lyrics about abortion, menopause, adultery, female sexuality, and the anguish of a suicidal mother's love for her daughters. In his estimation, her poetry was not sufficiently composed for a public audience and he told her, on more than one occasion, that she should give up what he referred to as her childish preoccupations, for she would surely outgrow them. While Holmes endorsed the writing of confessional poets, W. D. Snodgrass, George Starbuck, and Robert Lowell, he advised Sexton against publishing her work, warning her in harsh terms of the effects that difficult, unruly life narratives might unleash on her family.

Indeed, Sexton's subject matter and persona combined to violate the norms of what constituted a "civilized femininity" in post World War II suburban America. Her lecture notes, poetry, and public performances are fused with images of corporeal deviance that exceed the norms for being a good wife, obedient student, or respectful daughter. Sexton presents us with the image of an apparently disorderly woman whose poetry and teaching functions to widen the expressive options for women—offering them a means through which to articulate taboo emotions such as shame, grief, and ambivalence about motherhood and anxiety about the mutability of the body.

From the time Holmes first advised her not to publish *To Bedlam and Part Way Back,* a collection of poems about her suicidal breakdown, Sexton suspected that his disdain for her work was strained by his own self-deception—"In the long pull, John," she wrote in a letter that winter,

> Where you might be proud of me, you are ashamed of me. . . . I keep pretending not to notice. . . . But then, you remind me of my father (and I KNOW that's not your fault). But there is something else here. . . . Who do I remind you of? Whoever he or she was or is. . . . It isn't my fault. I am not they! (Perhaps I am all wrong, but I wish that you would consider this for a minute and remind yourself). (L. Sexton and Ames, 1977, 119)

The contempt that Holmes had for Sexton can easily be attributed to something more than a matter of taste. Holmes cast Sexton as an unruly student, a spectacle whose body was transgressive and most dangerous, precisely because her corporeal excess, addictions, and vulnerabilities resonated with his own demons, and these were matters he worked hard to forget. Holmes had been a "Jekyll-and-Hyde alcoholic" and prior to the 1950s, his life had been, as his widow described to Sexton's biographer, Diane Middlebrook, "ragged with horrors" (1991, 100). By the late 1950s, Holmes had stopped drinking, remarried, and established a life that was apparently secure and peaceful. Middlebrook speculates that his advice to Sexton was advice that he was given and had followed himself. Yet, while Holmes may indeed have intended to offer Sexton a strong dose of practical wisdom, he mistook what was best for him as being best for his student.

This form of self-deception—believing what is good for ourselves is good for our students—can suppress substantial differences between our students and ourselves. While we may have the best intentions when offering students our insights, orientations in taste, advice, recommendations or academic material, we may very well be sabotaging the possibilities for working with them to cultivate—through reading, writing, and deliberation of all sorts—their own internally persuasive voices, voices that can counter the larger cultural imperative to order, sameness, and hence, into monologism, narrowing the scope for representing and respecting otherness.[1]

In contrast, in *The Bonds of Love,* Jessica Benjamin (1998a) elaborates on the efficacy of what she refers to as *mutual recognition,* emphasizing that such mutuality short-circuits the will to subjugate the Other. Mutual recognition requires the balance of assertion and recognition (25). This state of mutuality, Benjamin says, is contingent on a capacity to experience the other as an active subject in his or her own right. If, for example, Sexton and Holmes were mutually to recognize one another, Holmes would not simply see Sexton as an extension of his own disavowed past. Nor would he demand that Sexton tame her professional desires and surrender to his assessment of her work and motives as a poet. Rather, both student and teacher would sustain a particular form of tension that enables them to take on what Benjamin describes as 'the double action of intersubjectivity—recognizing the other's subjectivity and one's own" (1998a, 24). Mapped onto pedagogy, this capacity would suggest that as the student becomes less objectified, the teacher becomes a more "subjective" subject (24). The relationship between John Holmes and Anne Sexton presents us with a perplexing example of a teacher–student relationship. On the surface, it might appear that Holmes offers us an example of a failed capacity to embody aspects of the "not-me," for he clearly felt that Sexton was an intrusive force that needed to be obliterated, to be cast "outside," and it was no secret that he lobbied the poetry community to stay away from her. However, a closer look at his history suggests otherwise. Holmes was so steeped in self-deception that he failed to recognize Sexton precisely because her past resonated so powerfully with a past he had disavowed, thus she summoned forth aspects of his self that he found painful and had worked to keep beyond the reach of his memory. Holmes represents Lacan's claim that the most intimate part of the psyche has the quality of being Other—a principle we will return to. Holmes does not offer a case of a teacher who cannot bear difference; rather he works as an exemplar of the cruel and aggressive actions we can take to perpetuate a sense of our own mastery and control in the face of what we cannot bear to recognize in ourselves—actions that perpetuate states of self-deception.

Sexton, on the other hand, offers us a clear case of a figure who has the capacity to attend to Holmes's point of view without foreclosing on her own poetic project. Why Sexton's work was so distasteful to him and why he was incapable of offering her a different sort of response is one of the subjects of this chapter, for I believe that it is important to consider the possibility that as teachers, writers, and researchers we may sometimes be more like Holmes than we dare imagine. What forms of self-forgetting do we rely on to sustain our sense of pedagogical authority? What vital lies do we rely on to create a sense of belonging, mastery, and intellectual well-being?

The concept of self-forgetting reflects larger cultural conflicts about the nature of the subjects we as teachers write about. It also affects how to regard these subjects, conflicts that pivot not simply on just how personal a subject should be, but which subjects are worthy of attention. As Anne Sexton's teacher, Holmes worked to bury the past while Sexton used what she learned from her teacher about writing poetry to cast light on family secrets that held significance on both a personal and social level. Once disclosed, Sexton believed that her inquiries might bring about what she describes in her poetic reply to Holmes—as a "certain sense of order." Sexton's subject matter is directed toward those intimate psychic truths that are often experienced as radically Other, truths she locates, as Elisabeth Bronfen (1998) goes on to explain, in the family romances her parents lived by, in the culture she was educated in (its fairy tales and myths), and in her unconscious life (293).

Alicia Ostriker (1988) echoes Bronfen's assessment of Sexton's pursuit of personal truth, noting that Sexton believed that knowing the truth about oneself, however devastating, can yield a pattern, a structure that will teach one "something worth learning" about how one's mysteries can be laid bare, how that which is intimate but opaque can be illuminated (263–287). The personal memories of madness and loss that Sexton rendered in her poetry are not *personal* as we conventionally understand it—private, interior, a mine to hoard, remember, or forget. She wrote in order to approach a more "authentic" existence, striving at every turn to listen more attentively to what remains inaudible or half-spoken in the interstices of the personal and the social. Sexton's creative writing pedagogy considers the subject as a social entity who works within the complexity of a community's politics structured through processes of inclusions and exclusions. Moreover, her writing and her pedagogy cannily staged what Bronfen describes as a psychoanalytic and a deconstructive truth: that the most interior part of the psyche, according to Jacques Lacan (in Miller, 1988), has a quality of being Other, of being like a parasitic foreign body, which he calls *extimacy*. Sexton's use of writing is precisely why Holmes accuses her of making a spectacle of herself, for the personal politics Sexton explores in her poetry challenge the normative notions of propriety in post–World War II America.

It is difficult to accept that we can take up specific practices that will magically lead us to self-awareness. People aren't that self-determined that they can be completely self-consciously transparent to themselves and control their doing. Language is not a transparent medium that works as a glass house of the soul, holding as it were, chambers of lies and chambers of truth. Given the limits of language, what forms of rhetorical authority can educators turn to that would minimize our proclivities for self-deception?

Rivaling, parody, concealment, and disappearance constitute a series of rhetorical tactics that offer Sexton in particular, and women in general, ways to make rival claims to forms of authority that fosters deception, fear, and betrayals. These rhetorical tactics have the capacity to create a more dynamic model of social subjectivity in the classroom that is directed toward mutual recognition. Because mutual recognition is contingent on a capacity to sustain one's ground while being attentive to the Other, we must consider the complexity of what it means to act autonomously within a nexus of intersubjective relationships.

To discuss these issues and explore the relationship between self-deception and teaching, take a close look at the correspondence Sexton and Holmes exchanged during the winter of 1961. Their correspondence is a limited case through which we can ponder our collective predicament as educators: What kind of pedagogical authority is obtained through self-deception? What forms of self-forgetting are we vulnerable to? And finally, what pedagogical practices can we draw on to expand the margin of awareness in our teaching lives to include a working through of the encrypted metaphors we live by as teachers?

AN OEDIPAL DRAMA REVISED

The year is 1957. Anne Sexton was twenty-nine years old. At the advice of her psychiatrist, Dr. Martin Orne, and despite acute episodes of anxiety that generally kept her bound to her house, Sexton decided to enroll in a poetry workshop at the Boston Center for Adult Education led by John Holmes. Sexton started in the middle of the term, bringing to the table a substantial collection of poems that she had been working on during the previous months. Holmes, a professor at Tufts University, was a kind, gentle man, deeply devoted to poetry and to teaching. In addition to being a well-respected poet, he reviewed books of poetry, taught poetry classes, and served as the president of the New England Poetry Club, which, under his direction, supported young poets and created occasions for promising writers to circulate their work.[2]

As a participant in Holmes's workshop, Sexton sat among eighteen other young, promising writers, praying, recalls Maxine Kumin, who also participated in this class, "that our poems would rise to the top of the pile under Professor Holmes' fingers as he alternately fussed with his pipe and shuffled pages, and one of us would thus be divinely elected for scrutiny" (Middlebrook, 1991, 51). Despite Sexton's lack of formal education, she did not feel out of place here. Rather, the atmosphere Holmes created felt quite unlike college, particularly, Sexton later recalled, because no one was competing "to get a good mark or to learn how to write a poem to satisfy a teacher." Later, Sexton recalls feeling at home in this workshop setting, as if she were among "her people." In an interview for the *Paris Review* in 1972, Sexton told Barbara Kevles that

the most important aspect for the class was that I felt I belonged somewhere. When I first got sick and became a displaced person, I thought I was quite alone, but when I went into the mental hospital, I found I wasn't, that there were other people like me. It made me feel better—more real, sane. I felt, "These are my people." Well, at the John Holmes workshop that I attended for two years, I found I belonged to the poets, that I was real there, and I had another "These are my people." I met Maxine Kumin, the poet and novelist, at that class. She is my closest friend. She is part superego, part sister, as well as pal of my desk. It's strange because we're quite different. She is reserved, while I tend to be flamboyant. She is an intellectual, and I seem to be a primitive. That is true about our poetry as well. (164)

Sexton learned many of what she referred to when teaching as her "tricks" in this course, a code term she used for composing smooth, complex stanzas with surprising internal rhymes (Middlebrook, 1991, 51). Holmes came to take on the status of a father figure, a censor, a professional influence, who guided her, writes Middlebrook, "in the task of speaking through a mask and valuing an air of distance and clever formal effects" (82). From Holmes, Sexton learned to write and to teach. "I learned to write from John, not Robert Lowell," she told Dr. Orne, after Holmes had died of cancer in 1962.

Growing out of the course at the Boston Adult Center for Education was a private poetry group that began to meet in the fall of 1958. Holmes, Sexton, Kumin, Sam Albert, and George Starbuck began to gather in one another's homes, rarely welcoming drop-ins, since the success of its procedures, writes Middlebrook, "depended on intimate knowledge of one another's work and respect for quite different artistic goals" (96). Yet, in the midst of the intimacy generated in this group, Holmes and Sexton were continually at odds with one another. For Holmes, who was all tweed and New England reserve, Sexton was excessive and at times rude and demanding. On a number of occasions, he expressed severe disapproval for the way she treated other poets in their group, and he warned Maxine Kumin that Sexton was a dangerous influence.

In 1958, Sexton was revising *To Bedlam and Part Way Back,* a collection of poems written about her nervous breakdown and attempted suicide. She brought it to her group for their response. Holmes felt disturbed by the poetry that Sexton was writing, fearing that it was far too personal. In a letter commenting on Sexton's manuscript, Holmes discusses her poetry in a manner he never before expressed:

> I distrust the very source and subject of a great many of your poems, namely all those that describe and dwell on your time in the hospital . . . it bothers me that you use poetry this way. It's all a release for you, but what is it for anyone else except a spectacle of someone experiencing release? . . . Don't publish it in a book. You'll certainly outgrow it, and become another person, and then this record will haunt and hurt you. It will even haunt and hurt your children, years from now. (qtd. in Middlebrook, 1991, 98–99)

No doubt, Sexton's writing touched an open nerve in Holmes. Not only did Holmes suffer with life-threatening episodes of alcoholism, but his first wife had committed a gruesome suicide. She had slashed her wrists and bled to death over all his papers, which she assembled for that purpose on his desk. "John never got over it," Kumin told Middlebrook, "and he feared the suicidal side of Anne" (110). While he tried to deny her talent, Sexton sought his respect. "She was desperately trying to make him into her Christian academic Daddy," Kumin recalls, "Anne had such a thing about authority figures. He would have none of that!" (100).

Throughout their relationship, Holmes reacted to Sexton with visceral intolerance, and in the case of *To Bedlam*, he directly accused her of using poetry to perform a spectacle of catharsis, ultimately casting Sexton as a contaminant to herself, her family, and the field. He continually tried to appeal to Kumin to rescue Sexton, and to help her to recognize what he believed to be serious limitations in her work (143). "I said way back," he wrote to Kumin, "that she was going to have a hard time to change subject matter, after the book, and it's true. . . . Not that she has two subjects, mental illness and sex, but that she writes so absolutely selfishly, of herself, to bare and shock and confess. Her motives are wrong, artistically, and finally the self-preoccupation comes to be simply damn boring" (143). Kumin did not adhere to Holmes's advice to stay away from Anne Sexton. Rather, they developed a close friendship that bound them until Sexton's death. They shared a continuous, daily collaboration on the telephone, leaving the receiver on their desks while working, cueing one another with a whistle when they needed to talk through a line or elicit from each other more and more work, more of what Kumin refers to as "furniture in the poems, more and more detail, more thickness of authenticity" (537). Kumin notes, "We really trained our ears that way. Because we were always hearing poems without seeing them, when I would see a Sexton poem at a workshop the following week, it would be quite startling to encounter it on the page" (537).

Kumin recognized the demands that Sexton placed on those who were close to her—she had desperate needs never to be left alone and to be constantly looked after. But Kumin has also said that, "Annie gave as good as she got . . . with Anne, I never felt I had to be anyone but myself, and I know she felt very much the same. There was a total acceptance of who were, and that is my fantasy of what sisters can have" (541–542). Unlike Holmes, Kumin did not fear being consumed or used by Sexton; she did not fear her sadness and longings; she was not terrified by the needs and appetites she had that couldn't be satisfied or by her psychotic breaks, trances, hallucinations, anger, or physical incapacitations. When asked in an interview if she felt that Sexton might pull her into the direction of bedlam, into the grip of psychosis, Kumin replied:

KUMIN: Oh no. I was hanging on to her, like the nuns who hung on to St. Theresa's boot tops to pull her back when she levitated. That was my relationship with Anne. I was trying very hard to keep her feet on the ground . . .

INTERVIEWER: Were you trying to save her in some way?

KUMIN: I don't know if I thought of it that way; I was just trying to root her. I was trying to keep her sane. . . . I'm still quite ambivalent about it . . . I . . . felt that rather than poetry being the catalyst that killed her, it was poetry that kept her alive. That I know full well.

In contrast to Holmes, who positioned Anne Sexton as the excessive and dangerous daughter, Kumin felt Sexton to be, as she said in a poem, "the sister I never had. She was *better* than any sister I could have had. It was the first relationship I had with someone of the same sex that was truly intimate bonding" (541). "One of the things I learned from my loving relationship with Anne," recalls Kumin, "was not to fear mental illness, not to be afraid of people who are in the grip of it. She was never anything but real to me. Even crazy, she was still Anne" (540). Kumin's refusal to distance herself from Sexton offers one clear case of love between women who forge a different sort of pedagogical encounter, one that can bear the weight of ambivalence and love and acknowledges rather than prohibits the dignity of the Other. Their friendship and collaboration portray the difference between the experience of being *with* another and being regulated by an Other (Benjamin, 1988, 46). In its most straightforward sense, the love between Sexton and Kumin might be characterized by the defining paradox of mutual recognition: sustaining a balance between recognition of the other and assertion of self. In her elaboration of this paradox, Benjamin makes some important distinctions between internalization and intersubjective theories. She notes that

> we have to get beyond internalization theory if we are to break out of the solipsistic omnipotence of the single psyche. The classic psychoanalytic viewpoint did not see differentiation as a balance, but as a *process of disentanglement.* Thus it cast experiences of union, merger, and self-other harmony as regressive opposites to differentiation and self-other distinction. Merging was a dangerous form of undifferentiation, a sinking back into the sea of oneness—the "oceanic feeling" that Freud told Romain Rolland he frankly couldn't relate to. The original sense of oneness was seen as absolute, as "limitless narcissism," and, therefore, regression to it would impede development and prevent separation. In its most extreme version, this view of differentiation pathologized the sensation of love: relaxing the boundaries of the self in communion with others threatened the identity of the isolate self. Yet this oneness was also seen as the ultimate pleasure, eclipsing the pleasure of difference. Oneness was not seen as a state that could coexist with (enhance and be enhanced by) the sense of separateness. One of the most important insights of intersubjective theory is that sameness and difference exist simultaneously in mutual recognition. (Benjamin, 1998, my emphasis)

Sexton's experiences of "being with" Kumin are predicated on the awareness they had of one another's differences—and the sense of intimacy they felt precisely because they were not fused together. "The externality of the other," notes Benjamin, "makes one feel one is truly being 'fed,' getting nourishment from the outside, rather than supplying everything for oneself" (92). The relationship between Kumin and Sexton foregrounds both the presence and the breakdown of mutual recognition that existed within this small and influential group of writers. Moreover, their relationship places in relief the potential price exacted when the differences within communities are experienced as an attack on the community's sense of mastery and cohesion.[3] Given that Holmes perceives Sexton as spoiling the group's solidarity by imposing her excessive and relentless workshop manners, she is positioned as failing, and her failings become the material for her teacher's subtle and insidious excessive self-regard. While Holmes ostensibly tries to set Sexton apart from the poetry group to protect members from being contaminated by her, his efforts also function to conceal from himself his own difficult memories.

In fact, not only does John Holmes position Sexton in ways that are beneficial to his project of forgetting, but his responses serve as a case in point of a melancholic strain that is distinctly masculine in its attempt to rescue poetry from Sexton and Sexton from herself, casting her as a mad and self-serving poet who must be avoided or, at the least, kept at a great distance. Also at stake is the fact that Holmes fails to recognize Sexton's losses and her point of view, while in his own poetry he masterfully appropriated the personal genre and surfaced as a "cultural hero." As a figure of the male, melancholic poet, Holmes denies symbolic expression of Sexton's own loss and grief, yet supports the "confessions" of such poets as George Starbuck and Robert Lowell. In the hands of male poets, loss and grief are powerful cultural properties, while for women, they yield little analytic possibilities. Lurking in John Holmes's disavowal of Anne Sexton's writing and in his concerns that her writing was too personal, and nothing more than a release that she would surely outgrow, are traces of his own disowned counterparts and his failure to withstand the contingencies between his life and that of Anne Sexton.

Adam Phillips (1994) observes that within all our lives, there are areas that we pretend to lose or that never evolve because they are unacceptable or unbearable, consequently we hide them from ourselves. The most profound way of recognizing something, or the only way to recognize some things, notes Phillips in his gloss of Freud's 1926 work on inhibitions, is through practices of concealing things from us. "And what is profound," writes Phillips, "or rather of interest, is not only what one has hidden but also the ways one has of hiding it" (1993, 17). Phobias, obsessions, and repressions offer us a means through which to conceal difficult memories, for they provide us with places to harbor a secret life, a place to hide unbearable self-knowledge. The hiding places we construct enable us to hoard the past and keep ourselves from coming to know its import. Phillips suggests that we mislay difficult memories for what we might think of as aesthetic reasons; they are felt to be incompatible with whatever we believe to be good or desirable for or about ourselves (22). Given this framework, a mislaid memory functions as an obscure but crucial clue to what we believe constitutes a good life. Phillips' discussion of Freud's notion of aesthetics and judgment is of direct relevance to the larger discussion of memory and forgetting. Phillips goes on to point out, according to Freud, that judgment, or aesthetic valuation, is fundamentally a question of whether something is edible. In talking this way about judgment, Freud is, by implication, also talking about memory and forgetting.

> [T]he judgment is, "I should like to eat this," or "I should like to spit it out"; and, put more generally: "I should like to take this into myself and to keep that out". That is to say, "it shall be inside me" or "it shall be outside me" . . . the original pleasure-ego wants to introject into itself everything that is good and to eject from itself everything that is bad. What is bad, what is alien to the ego and what is external are, to being with, identical. (23)

Thus, argues Phillips, Freud is not only rendering his paradigm for judgment, he is describing two forms of forgetting as well. The question raised by Phillips goes like this: Is forgetting more like eating something or like spitting it out? Just as we can only repress something once we have recognized it, so we can only spit something out once we have tasted it. If you spit something out, you eliminate it once and for all; if you eat something, you forget it through a process of digestion. Spat out it will have to be metabolized by a world that you have exempted yourself from; taken in, it will be metabolized by your body and fuel your future (23). The point is, suggests Phillips, not what do I want to remember or forget, but *what forms of forgetting do I want to use?* (my emphasis).

It appears John Holmes spit out the anguish of his wife's suicide and the terror and disgust he felt during his days of alcoholism and depression, projecting what he came to find so distasteful onto Sexton, struggling, albeit, unsuccessfully, to put these emotions beyond the reach of his memory. Yet, is it possible to completely spit out our memories?

This sketch of a teacher and student can be read as a cryptogram that touches on but does not make manifest the meaning inherent in the anxiety, rage, and in the plaints that Holmes lodged against Sexton, all of which represent his attempts to "cure" her of bad taste. To what extent, we must ask ourselves, do our cultural endeavors as teachers work to exact similar effects on our students? Can we conclude that Holmes's relationship with Sexton brought about an uncanny reunion with painful areas of his own life, and in an effort to keep these areas beyond the reach of his memory he not only denied her recognition, splitting the poetry workshop into good and evil, but he portrays how a teacher who takes such a route to establishing his own authority and power can potentially create an absence that results in a profound sense of lack where the Other should be?[4] To what extent do Holmes's responses to Sexton represent the potential danger that can ensue when we fail to work through our losses? What I haven't fully addressed thus far are Sexton's responses to John Holmes. Her extended replies offer us an exemplum for working toward the reflected separation that mutual recognition is so contingent on, a process that offers lessons in possessing one's own mind in the presence of others. But before we attend to Sexton's response to John Holmes, consider the narcissistic strains in his letter, for these strains undermine his capacity for recognizing her talent as well as potentially thwart Sexton's poetic project.

The Shadow of Narcissism

I do not intend to treat narcissism as a pathological category or a wound that should incite shame. Narcissism haunts each of us. In his discussion of Eastern spirituality and psychoanalysis, psychiatrist Mark Epstein explains that "the Buddha sees us all as Narcissus, gazing at and captivated by our own reflections, languishing in our attempted self-sufficiency" (1995, 48). Narcissism deeply divides us, for part of what the narcissist cannot bear is his or her inner conflict, difference, and sense of vulnerability. This is precisely what appears to have been difficult for John Holmes as Sexton brought him face to face with inner tensions that he had yet to resolve. Like many of us, Holmes appears to have cast his disowned counterparts beyond the pale, only to find his history of loss return to him in the presence of Anne Sexton. The story of Holmes and Sexton offers one possible account of how the strategies teachers often use to recover from narcissistic wounds can be cruel, aggressive, and tie them to habits of self-deception.[5] What moves do teachers and students make to compensate for these wounds? Where do they turn for consolation? In which identifications do they find solace?

While the teacher's capacity to control, predict, and measure is not, as Deborah Britzman aptly points out, ordinarily associated with the psychic demands of narcissism, the dynamics underlying the pull to be certain and to control indeed set in motion forms of anxiety that make it unthinkable to understand or gain insight without recourse to mastery (1998, 26). Holmes's impulse to control Sexton surfaces throughout their correspondences. Recall that he does not simply advise Sexton not to publish *To Bedlam*; he additionally plays the role of seer and makes two predictions: that Sexton will outgrow this work, and that this record will return to haunt and hurt her children years from now. Far more than self-love or excessive self-regard, narcissism is, argues Bela Grunberger, "an omnipotent feeling of absolute autonomy, of faultless perfection . . . and a spontaneous tendency toward expansion, a feeling of boundlessness, of eternity" (1989, 167). This sense of confidence is inspired by a relentless desire for purity, that is, a desire to be unencumbered by the demands of others who might interfere with our self-aggrandizing impulses or our pull to craft visions of perfection. Thus, writes Britzman, the dynamic of narcissism provokes questions of value. Holmes not only questions the value of Sexton's poetry, but he expresses what she describes in a letter to him as a "criticism of her as a person"—a criticism that devalues her work so profoundly that it pierces her to the bone. In a letter responding to Holmes's concerns, Sexton admits that "I didn't say that your criticism of me was perceptive, but bitter, or that I would like to cry and that I felt ashamed" (59).

Holmes's move to control his truant past involved a form of forgetting that gathered force and compelled him to project or spit out what he believed to be impure within himself onto Sexton, in turn rendering her as an extension of himself rather than as a person who is separate, who stands apart and offers a different point of view. This desire sabotaged the possibility for mutual recognition. We might understand this act of projection as a response to the profound sense of loss that he had yet to grieve—the loss of alcohol, the loss of his former wife to suicide, the loss of a past that alters his present history, and the loss of a future. Each of these losses combines to alert us to narcissistic issues, for the passing of time is not only intrinsically traumatic, but it wakes us up, as psychoanalyst Christopher Bollas (1994) reminds us, to our inevitable finitude, mortality, and physical, intellectual, and emotional vulnerabilities. If narcissism is dependent on a sense of faultless perfection and a feeling of boundlessness, then the recognition of limitations that are imposed by chronological time and the materiality of the body, its impurities and inevitable decay, is indeed experienced as narcissistic wounds. The narcissistic strain in Holmes's response to Sexton's aesthetic is not only tied to loss and a recognition of limits, but that fears of contamination and desires for clean confessions articulated by proper bodies are tied to narcissistic wounds. These wounds manifest themselves in anxieties about corporeal deviance and bodily disappearance. I suggest that we read education's anxieties about bodies that deviate from the norm—whether they are bodies that are physically disabled or bodies whose emotional life is "hard to read" and thus challenge the pragmatic structure of the classroom—as symptomatic of a narcissistic wound associated with fears of contamination, a desire for perfection, and a compulsion to impose a normative sense of order on things.

The themes running through the story of Sexton and Holmes include those of gender, bodily disappearance, anxieties about corporeal vulnerability, and fears of feeling lost in our own lives or separated from those we love. My persistent return to the Anne Sexton archive provides me with the most lucid examples of how particular stories simply come and take us; they occupy us; they demand that we work out, again and again, what they mean, and the meaning held in our obsessions with them. Perhaps the most obvious theme in the limited case of Sexton and Holmes, however, is about writing and the ways in which writing can be used to illuminate those aspects of self-deception that we rely on to sustain our sense of pedagogical authority. Here, writing is a social form, for I am most interested in what Carolyn Steedman terms "writing in society." "Writing," notes Steedman, "connotes form and function. That is to say, as an idea it must continually draw our attention to the way in which, as a material process and a technology, it places constraints on us (*it is not the same as speech-written-down; it is not a transcription of spoken language*) (1992, my emphasis). As a project, writing must continually spell out both restraint and permission, must draw our attention to the literary forms available to people in different historical epochs, forms that sometimes restrain the writing of the self, sometimes permit it (Steedman, 1992, 14).

If writing, as Steedman asserts, is a social form through which "the self is written out of and into its historical context," then I suggest that we attend to the price exacted when a writer uses the autobiographical *I* to enter the historical field. Writers use skilled rhetorical maneuvers to mitigate the price of exposure, for autobiographical writing can threaten writers with unsympathetic scrutiny. In the context of the classroom, public and private life can combine to provoke shame or legitimization in our students. Consequently, it is not surprising that writers might be ambivalent about transferring private matters into public discourse, thereby using writing as a means of concealment as well as revelation. Perhaps Sexton's repeated insistence that she keeps secrets and that she likes to hide worked as a rhetorical strategy for calling attention to the social and political constraints in which she wrote.

As described in chapter 1, Sexton often used her lectures at Colgate University to "talk back" to her critics. In this particular lecture on autobiography, Sexton admits to her students that while she leads her readers to believe that she is an autobiographical poet, she uses the personal, the autobiographical *I*, to, in her words, "apply a mask to my face somewhat like a young man applying the face of an aging clown." She goes on:

> Picture me at my dressing table for a moment putting on the years. All those nights, all those cups of coffee, all those sneezes, all those shots of bourbon at 2 A.M. . . . all this applied like a rubber mask that the robber wears . . . when I tell you this poem is about Daphne, please remember that I am lying. You will hear me tell you that often. I like to lie. I like to confess. I like to hide.[6]

Perhaps Sexton's insistence that she likes to hide is in fact a means by which she underscores the ways in which her writing spells out restraint and disclosure to her readers. I imagine that what is implied in her calculated assertion of hiding and disclosure goes something like this: "I can write from a personal position because the personal has been sanctioned by post–World War II culture and society—specifically by male poets such as George Starbuck and Robert Lowell. However, what I can express as a female poet remains limited. Thus, to write about the anguish of failing to care for my children, the depth of my psychic struggles and loneliness, requires that I hide behind a mask, a personae. I know that the price exacted in representing such anguish may very well result in exclusion from the very community that has offered me intellectual and emotional strength. To protect myself, I intermingle fiction with autobiography—in short, I invent as much as I represent."

The price of exposure that the autobiographical writer may potentially pay has been one of the central concerns of educators who have been critical of bringing personal writing into the classroom. In her essay, "Interrupting the Calls for Student Voice in 'Liberatory' Education: A Feminist Poststructuralist Perspective," Mimi Orner (1992) locates the problem of exposure in what she describes as the "hidden curriculum of the talking circle—the long cherished form of the democratic classroom." The talking circle that Sexton was a part of in Holmes's workshop indeed contained a hidden curriculum, one that made implicit demands on Anne Sexton to discipline herself in ways that matched Holmes's standards for propriety and expression. As Sexton became more resistant and critical of these implicit standards, Holmes became more and more inclined to pathologize her for not adhering to his advice about what to exclude from her poetry and what to lay bare. We might speculate that given Holmes's history with suicide and addiction, he felt one or two degrees removed from the ideal of the rational, esteemed poet and husband. Given his precarious standing, he may have felt more invested in presenting and defending ideals of sobriety, and in disguising or presenting himself as a reasonable man.

As I read through the case of Sexton and Holmes, I became more interested in the ways in which we may use writing and teaching as a means to hide difficult truths about ourselves. Why, for example, do I use the story of Sexton to speak about writing, pedagogy, curriculum theory and gender—why do I turn to someone else's narrative rather than my own?[7] Recognizing Holmes's transferences onto Sexton placed in relief questions about my own transferences onto her.

Like so many female scholars before me, I turn to an author who is distant, dead. My old notebooks are full of women writers who are at war with life: Orianna Fallaci, Virginia Woolf, Lillian Helman, Zelda Fitzgerald, women who loved and wrote, women who had big appetites, women taken with passion, women like Irene Vilar who also keeps notebooks of women writers at war with life. Vilar likens herself to the Chilean Violeta Parra, who wrote the song "Gracias a la Vida," a writer who killed herself later, in stages, like my father, like Hellman, like Sexton, like Fitzgerald, not immediately, but slowly, with alcohol. Why do I elect to turn, not to a living woman, but to her work, her legacy? Why did I turn away from the living women in my everyday life to learn lessons about teaching and writing, and the psychic work required to understand my teaching life? I defied, in effect turned away from, what Teresa de Laurentis (1987) describes as a sense of "entrustment" with the women I love and work with. De Lauretis characterizes this relationship as one in which "one woman gives her trust or entrusts herself symbolically to another woman, who thus become her guide, mentor, or point of reference. Both women engage in the relationship ... not in spite but rather because and in full recognition of the disparity that may exist between them" (32). "Women's trust," as Carolyn G. Heilbrun notes in a gloss of de Laurentis's text, "is not incompatible with unequal power" (1988, 37). Perhaps in my studies of Anne Sexton's teaching life, I sought out lessons in entrustment, lessons in the difficult work of mutual recognition, lessons that I found in the relationship Sexton shared with Kumin and, through her work at the Radcliffe Institute in 1962 with Tillie Olsen, a poet who generously offered Sexton a language for failure.[8]

Leigh Gilmore reminds her readers that implicit in the project of autobiography is a desire to become other than who one is—that the longing that fuses the autobiographical *I* is a longing for self transformation (2001, 11). Gilmore suggests that we think about autobiography as a site of theory. Taking a cue from Valery's dictim that "every theory is the fragment of an autobiography," Gilmore suggests that we consider the fragments of theory that are embodied within autobiography. For Gilmore, "autobiography is an assembly of theories of the self and self-representation; of personal identity and one's relation to a family, a region, a nation; and of citizenship and a politics of representativeness (and exclusion)" (12). The task of autobiography, as Gilmore goes on to propose, is to address the larger organizational questions that pertain to how to represent personal experiences that challenge a social milieu's notion of what constitutes health and well-being. Sexton's use of personae and masks offers her readers and her students a set of rhetorical strategies for representing the selves that we are inclined to ignore or disavow. Moreover, as implied in Sexton's lecture notes, the protective sheath of a mask can bring us to the limits of conventional autobiography and illuminate what such narratives often obscure (Pagano, 1991).

The Unconscious Father

It is likely that I may very well have played the good student in the eyes of John Holmes, for I, too, harbor anxieties about unruly narratives. I suspect that I would have taken his advice and decided not to air my family secrets. Perhaps Holmes may have been cautioning Sexton to remember that narratives exact a price in the telling. No matter how tightly composed, ordered, or restrained, narratives surpass the conscious intent of the writer—they are participatory acts, occurring at the level of intersubjective relationships, and so they contain a surplus of the unforeseen, of self-exposure, a kind of communicative alchemy that can be as historically recuperative or redemptive as it can be transformative or personally strengthening. Thus, much of my ambivalence about personal writing is tied to the concussive quality of narrative: narratives can shock and linger; they can astonish or position our students in ways that can summon respect, understanding, shame, or sorrow. And there is always the risk that what is narrated cannot be ethically attended to, particularly if the teacher cannot bear the weight of the student's message.

While Holmes was a loving and gentle teacher, his urge to control and purify Sexton's disclosures belies unreflected anxieties that threatened to limit Sexton's education as a poet in very significant ways. Throughout this limited case, Holmes plays out the fate of the unconscious father, a figure who bears a striking resemblance to the father described by Lacan in his *Ecrits*. Lacan (1977) argues that the true formula for atheism is not that God is dead, but that God is unconscious. In the context of the Oedipal drama, Lacan offers us not a dead father but an unconscious one; a father who is unaware and does not know that he is dead, which, on a figurative level, suggests that he sleeps in an effort to avoid the deadliness of an answer, "of a knowing that kills" (Gilmore, 2001, 158). This is a variation of Lacan's portrayal of the unconscious father, for the issue at stake, which is the knowledge that Holmes apparently "closes his eyes to," is his own corporeal vulnerability. Holmes's lapse of consciousness creates scenes full of pathos as he positions Sexton as the daughter who does not know [better], and implores her to read her body of work through his eyes, to accept his analysis, and, thus, to protect his narcissistic ties to mastery. While Sexton holds pathos in prompts like, "What is it [your poetry] for anyone except a spectacle of someone experiencing release," Holmes appears as the intellectually certain teacher who will deliver his student from evil. Sexton was all too aware, as she once told Barbara Kevles in an interview, that Holmes saw her as something evil (Kevles, 1972). Perhaps in searching, as Kumin once noted, for a "Christian academic Daddy," Sexton was searching for a father who possessed a particular form of consciousness that made it possible for mutual recognition to emerge—for within Catholicism, God sustains consciousness in the face of his son's anguished struggle with truth and justice, virtue, sin, and desire.[9] This figure of the father was no doubt compelling to Sexton, considering that she converted to Catholicism at the end of her life. It may have been, however, that Sexton was seeking a figure of authority who had the ethical stamina to offer a respectful reading of her work, a teacher who could bear the weight of her message as her Jewish academic "sister" Maxine Kumin did.

This brings us to another important crossroad in our study of Sexton and Holmes. What makes it possible for a teacher to bear the weight of her student's message? What messages put us to sleep? What conditions undermine the teacher's capacity to sustain consciousness? What is particularly significant about the relationship between Holmes and Sexton is that despite his criticism of her, despite his apparent failure to sustain the conscious awareness necessary for mutual recognition to take hold, he did not undermine her poetic project.

Sexton insisted on using her poetry to "inquire further," that is, to provoke questions about the strength of reason that resides in bodies that hold and articulate sorrow, that long for but cannot quite sustain sobriety or attach to meaning or to life. "I didn't say," wrote Sexton in the same letter to Holmes, "that poetry has saved my life; has given me a life and if I hadn't wandered in off the street and found you and your class, that I would indeed be lost" (1959, 59). Sexton did not defy her teacher, nor did she completely disregard his criticisms of her. Rather, Sexton offered Holmes a rival claim that took the form of a letter and a poem, "For John, Who Begs Me Not to Inquire Further." Portions of the letter read as follows (L. Sexton and Ames, 1977, 59–60):

[To John Holmes, possible draft]
[40 Clearwater Road] Lincoln's Birthday
[1959]

Dear John,

I have spent the morning writing you a poem. . . . And now that's that. . . . Of course there are other poems that I did not write. I didn't say that, although we seem to be strangers that I wave to you from my distant shore, that I send semaphore signals that you might find my signal no matter how foreign the language. I didn't say that you have taught me everything I do know about poetry, and taught me with firm patience and a kind smile. I didn't say that I have spent two years wishing that you would like me and feeling instinctively you did not. I didn't say how I cried the day this summer after leaving your house, because you were such a good man and your home seemed to radiate. I didn't say that I am surely a fan of yours, a lesser but a firm fan. I didn't say how welcome you make me feel in your home when you think to include me to a party.

This letter suggests that Sexton cultivated a growing capacity to rival an authority figure in such a way as to sustain an appreciation for Holmes's kindness while at the same time refused to disavow the value of her work. Later in this letter, Sexton addresses Holmes's concerns that she will change and then regret publishing her work. "Of course, I will shuck off this shell," she writes. "Of course I will change, will grow to look around instead of inside. But in case it takes a little while, I hope that you will wave back to me from your distant shore, and understand the signal—if not the words, will see the gesture and disregard the lack of sound" (L. Sexton, 1977, 59). Sexton's "gestures" to Holmes articulate a revisionary ethos that challenges his attempt to erase her body of work. Not only does Sexton exhibit a revisionary temperament in this letter but she demonstrates a capacity to attune to another's body and point of view, despite the threat it poses to her own project—each of which is necessary for cultivating mutual recognition.

Rhetorically, *rivaling* is a literate practice in which people explore open questions through an analysis of multiple and often conflicting perspectives and evidence. What is not addressed in discussions of rivaling are the particular emotional capacities necessary to pursue such analysis.[10] These capacities are relevant to our larger discussion of the role that mutual recognition can play in pedagogy. Rivaling is not merely a persuasive contest that yields a winner; rather it is a form of inquiry that permits all participants to demonstrate agency, giving forms to multiple points of view. This practice has its analogue in mutual recognition, placing in relief an important aspect of intersubjective theory that permits us to distinguish between two people who recognize one another from one person who regulates the other (Benjamin, 1998b, 45). A rival claim that is generative alters our expectations or "returns a difference"—giving us insight into our lives that, while intimate, may have remained opaque to us (Elsworth, 1997). R. H. Ennis defines the kind of critical thinking associated with rivaling as dependent not just on abilities (such as parsing an argument for claims, reasons, conclusion, or using logic) but on dispositions that predispose one to be open-minded, to consider points of view that challenge one's own, and to reason from premises with which one does not agree (qtd. in Flower, 2000, 42). Throughout this limited case, Sexton shows a growing capacity to engage with positions quite different from her own while at the same time sustain the integrity of her work. However, Sexton does not exemplify a form of "critical thinking" that follows from the perspective of formal, logical patterns of consistency; rather, her approach to rivaling her teacher rests on resisting and transforming the status quo. Her letter to him and her poetic response uncover the ideological dominance and exercise of power that Holmes sought to exert on their writing workshop, all of which he exerted to conceal from himself his own intellectual and emotional vulnerabilities.

Sexton lays bare her feelings toward Holmes—she does not cast him as an angry father—nor does she disappear from sight—putting her poetry to rest in a drawer, taking on his fears that her writing will return to hurt and haunt her family years from now. Her decision to question Holmes's position offered her teacher and her readers the possibility of incorporating figures of corporeal deviance into their visions of oppositional identities that exceed the norms for being a good mother, daughter, student, and female artist in post–World War II America. The bodies in *To Bedlam* are broken; they are stiff with fear and lost in what Sexton describes as the "inward look that society scorns" (Sexton, 1960). Holmes failed to recognize that the aim of Sexton's poetry was not only an avowal of her most intimate feelings, but also, as Bronfen (1998) argues, a series of renderings of "the more painful aspects of female experience in all its most horrific intensity" (296). Given the psychic content of Sexton's poetry and given the history of John Holmes, it is not surprising that he would collapse Sexton's poetry into her life. His reading, however, overlooks the fact that her poetry makes evident the distance between the female poet, her body, and the poetic text itself. Throughout Sexton's lecture notes, as I discussed in chapter 1, she argues that she does not use writing to confess; rather, she performs or plays at confession. Bronfen describes the deviant, vulnerable bodies in Sexton's poetry as a series of rhetorical gestures that present readers with what they may think is a woman in all her intimacy confessing her private desires, fantasies, and anxieties. "You do see this," notes Bronfen, "but you are also presented with a text of feminine intimacy, a duplicitous representation of the feminine confession, in fact a self-conscious performance of the fact that we are performatively constructed according to the stories we are taught and the stories we live by" (297). Thus, one potential rhetorical consequence of Sexton's poetry was not only to use her addicted, anguished, and melancholic middle-class body as a thematic subject of her poetry as well as a poetic medium, but also to use her body to compose poetic personae that bring us face to face with narcissistic attachments to idealized, rational, self-regulated bodies. And this sheds some important light on the issues under discussion about the challenge of mutual recognition because this psychic process challenges us as teachers not only to recognize alternative perspectives, but also to develop a capacity to attune ethically to bodies that may indeed challenge our narcissistic attachments. In the following section, we take a closer look at the aggressive and at time cruel strategies that Holmes used to recover from his own narcissistic wounds, noting the implications his responses have for teaching poetry as a form of composition that engages teachers and students in the challenge of mutual recognition.

"SOMETHING WORTH LEARNING . . . IN THE COMMONPLACES OF THE ASYLUM"

It was no secret to Anne Sexton that John Holmes disapproved of her. When asked how John Holmes felt about her poetry, Sexton responded quite frankly:

> During the years of that class, John Holmes saw me as something evil and warned Maxine to stay away from me. He told me I shouldn't write such personal poems about the madhouse. He said, "This isn't a fit subject for poetry." I knew no one who thought it was; even my doctor clammed up at that time. I was on my own. I tried to mind them. I tried to write the way the others, especially Maxine, wrote, but it didn't work. I always ended up sounding like myself. (Kevles, 1972, 166)

Sexton and Holmes differed on a number of counts, including workshop manners. She liked to promote more open discussion about the poems at the table, creating a space in which participants might explore where an image came from or what associations it generated. George Starbuck, in recalling the years when he was a member of this workshop, admitted that

> None of us in this group was the psychiatrist kind of workshop teacher, poem teacher; we didn't try to do the kind of thing Anne later learned to do as a teacher—insistently but noncoercively asking simple little questions about where does this come from, how did you dream this up, how old were you when this first happened to you. I was, and Max was, much more interested in tricks and wordplay. (qtd. in Middlebrook, 1991, 98)

Holmes, however, preferred a more directly focused discussion. His approach in the workshop clashed with Sexton's, which fed on "an unbridled excitement that would fuse the group process and lead to frequent and inspired revision" (qtd. in Middlebrook, 1991, 141). "This is a great strength and a great, but mutual intuitive creative act each time it happens" fumed Sexton to Holmes after he had written her his disapproving letter about their behavior that evening in 1961, "to repress the process would be to kill the work." While Holmes claimed that her rude treatment of another writer attending the workshop was intolerable, Sexton knew that there was more to his anger than their different approaches to working on a poem. In the letter that Sexton wrote to Holmes about her behavior that night, I want to attend to the open questions Sexton poses to her teacher. She does not try to persuade Holmes of her point of view, nor does she summarize his accusations about her. Rather, she raises a series of open questions that involve her exploring her own assumptions—implicating herself as much as Holmes in this painful riff between them. Throughout this letter, Sexton asserts her own authority by articulating sensitive insights that she was capable of pursuing given her extensive background in psychoanalysis. She writes: "In the long pull John, where you might be proud of me, you are ashamed of me. I keep pretending not to notice.... But then you remind me of my father (and I KNOW that's not your fault. But there is something else here.... who do I remind you of"?

What Sexton came to learn from Holmes, as Middlebrook so astutely points out, is how, despite his role as the critical, disapproving censor, to negoti-ate a substantial critical establishment that lodged similar critiques at her work. Sexton in fact remapped the Oedipal complex as a simple desire for the father. Her response to Holmes's warning not to publish *To Bedlam* took the form of an *apologia* poem she titled "To John, Who Begs Me Not to Inquire Further." This poem served not only as a defense of her poetry, but of the genre of con-temporary confessional writing with which she was associated. In the classic account of the Oedipal complex, the girl forgets her desire for her mother and aligns herself with the law of the father, refusing to *inquire further,* a line Sex-ton takes from a letter Schopenhauer wrote to Goethe. Schopenhauer quotes Jocasta, who begs Oedipus "not to inquire further." The following quote from Sexton's letter captures the spirit of "indefatigable enquiry" that Sexton pursued through writing, despite its costs. She writes:

> It is the courage to make a clean breast of it in the face of every question that makes the philosopher. He must be like Sophocles's Oedipus, who, seeking enlightenment concerning his terrible fate, pursues his indefatigable enquiry, even when he divines that appalling horror awaits him in the answer. But most of us carry in our heart the Jocasta who begs Oedipus for God's sake, not to inquire further.[11]

Bollas's spin on the Oedipal drama suggests that the "achievement" of the Oedipal complex is that the child inherits or wakes up to point of view: "I'm not only my mother's son and possible lover, but also my father's, and my mother looks different from my father's point of view and so forth" (Bollas, 1994, 159). In this account, the super ego announces not one but multiple perspectives. In this sense, we might speculate that the limited case of Sexton and Holmes also offers us an exemplum, not of an Oedipal drama, but of what Benjamin describes as "post-oedipal complementarity." In this phase, persons can tolerate the tension of opposing desires and identifications. "In effect," notes Benjamin, "accepting the very incompleteness of each position makes multiple positions possible: not precisely identifying with all positions at once, but aware of their possibility. This awareness allows a fuller symbolization, one that ... bridges rather than splits opposites such as active and passive" (1998, 33).

In the poem, "For John, Who Begs Me Not to Inquire Further," Sexton renders a series of images that depict an inquiry into the commonplaces of madness. Here, she locates perspectives, that, while distasteful to many, are invaluable to her. Sexton includes such lines in this poem, as

> Not that it was beautiful,
> but, that, in the end, there was
> a certain sense of order there;
> something worth learning
> in that narrow diary of my mind,
> in the commonplaces of the asylum
> where the cracked mirror
> or my own selfish death
> outstared me. . . .

Sexton refuses to incorporate the constricting norms that Holmes tried to hold her to, hence moving against potential subordination. We are all vulnerable to the influence of powerful figures. "If we are to oppose the abuses of power," argues Judith Butler "(which is not the same thing as opposing power itself), it seems wise to consider in what ways our vulnerability to that abuse consists" (1997, 20). Butler adds that our vulnerability consists precisely in seeking recognition in terms, names, and conventions that are not of our own making, but that we have inherited and that hold political and epistemic weight. The scenes I rendered of Sexton and Holmes illustrate how she at once pursued a kind of subordination, seeking a "Christian academic Daddy," in an effort to secure a promise of her existence in a world in which she continually felt displaced. At the same time, these scenes illustrate a male poet who, like Oedipus, fails to recognize the value of multiple points of view. Perhaps by returning to the scene of the madhouse, where points of view that counter norms and conventions are found, Sexton is able to loosen Holmes's grip on her. At the same time, she comes face to face with the ways in which madness and sanity, the personal and the private, are not distinctly different realms; rather, they are contingent on one another for definition.

A pedagogy that addresses contingency is arranged around a set of politicized preoccupations that pertain, but are not limited to, bodily disappearance, corporeal vulnerability, and remembrance in the face of loss. The practice of contingency addresses the anxious desire we feel in the face of loss not to be separated from whom or what is now absent. Most important, like John Holmes, the critics of Anne Sexton failed to recognize that the task of reading, writing, and teaching auto(bio)graphy require, as Nancy Miller (1991) points out, that we learn to discern the texture and the elements of our own experiences, our own sharp, blank, agonizing instability—beneath the imprint of another in order to move on. "But to do this," Miller goes on to say, "requires first recognizing the radical separateness of the other's design, the sound of another's voice; to do this in the classroom may require writing it down for others to hear" (469). Through such life-writing practices, we might begin to remake the names and conventions that we have inherited, thereby loosening their grip on us and bring us closer to recognizing Others as well as the Others within ourselves.

1. Anne Sexton with her husband, Alfred Muller Sexton II ("Kayo"), at Harvard University, 1968, receiving membership in the Harvard Chapter of Phi Beta Kappa. She is the first woman to receive this award. Courtesy of the Harry Ransom Humanities Research Center.

2. Anne Sexton with students, Marietta College, Ohio. Courtesy of the Harry Ransom Humanities Research Center.

3. Anne Sexton at Rockland Community College, New York, October 22, 1969. Courtesy of the Harry Ransom Humanities Research Center.

4. Anne Sexton at Marquette University, April 27, 1970. Courtesy of the Harry Ransom Humanities Research Center.

5. Anne Sexton at Tufts University, 1970, receiving an honorary degree. Courtesy of the Harry Ransom Humanities Research Center.

6. Anne Sexton at Harvard University, 1968. Courtesy of the Harry Ransom Humanities Research Center.

7. Linda and Mommie, 1961 or 1962. Courtesy of the Harry Ransom Humanities Research Center.

8. Anne Sexton and Linda Gray Sexton, approx. 1970. Courtesy of the Harry Ransom Humanities Research Center.

9. Anne Sexton posing for a publicity photograph with her husband, Kayo and daughters, Linda and Joy, 1961. Photograph courtesy of the *Boston Globe*.

CHAPTER FOUR

"... [I] Bend Down My Strange Face to Yours, And Forgive You"

A Study of Anne Sexton's Pedagogy of Reparation

What she couldn't give me, she made sure I got from someone else.

—*Joy Sexton, Anne Sexton's daughter*

A FAMILY PORTRAIT

Sunday, October 6, 1974. Anne Sexton has been dead for two days. She is remembered in the New York Times as "a disciple of Robert Lowell ... a confessional poet who fashioned art out of anguish. ... A forty-seven year old woman ... recently divorced from her husband, found dead in an idling car from a possible suicide ... leaving behind two daughters, Linda Gray and Joyce Ladd."

Sexton had a particular purchase on the image of the suicidal female poet who failed as a mother and wife. In a 1961 family publicity photograph taken for the *Boston Globe* that includes Joy, Linda, Sexton, and her husband, Kayo, we are faced with some popular images of suburban life. At first, this photograph, taken only four years after Sexton's first suicide attempt in 1957, appears to be a typical, middle-class domestic scene. It is a memento of the past that offers a record that can be read in several ways. Kayo, dressed in a dark suit and tie, takes the traditional place as "wife"—he sits behind Sexton, who somewhat seductively looks into the camera, holding a copy of her newest collection of poems, *All My Pretty Ones*. Her gaze suggests an appetite for something that lies beyond the confines of domestic responsibilities. This shot includes a background of shelves neatly lined with books. Sexton wears a fitted, white V-neck knit sweater and black-and-white striped skirt. A barometer hangs on the wall behind Kayo. Within the frame of this publicity photograph is another smaller photograph—a head shot of Sexton. This small photograph appears on the back cover of her book. In both images, Sexton looks directly out, toward her audience, while Kayo, Joy, and Linda gaze down, toward the pages of *All My Pretty Ones* as if they are looking at a family photo album.

But there is more. Linda's eyes are rimmed with dark circles. If you frame her face, you might detect a sense of sadness in her expression, perhaps fear. Eight-year-old Linda looks aged, worn. If we look closer at her expression, we can see the effects of living in the Sexton household in 1961. These effects are registered in the pallid tone of her skin, the hesitancy in her smile. In Linda's memoir, *Searching for Mercy Street: A Journey Back to My Mother,* she remembers one weeknight in autumn, when she was eight. A dinner of calves' liver and baked potatoes is over. Sexton is sitting at the table, smoking, twirling her hair, and, as Linda recalls, "stirring the melting ice in her martini with her finger" (1994, 43). This evening, there will be a violent fight that begins because Sexton wants eight-year-old Linda to do the dishes. Kayo becomes angry. He accuses Sexton of "just not wanting to do them herself." Their "discussion," which is the family euphemism for "fight," deteriorates. And in the midst of their arguing, Sexton screams at Kayo, "Go ahead and hit me. It'd be a relief to have you kill me" (45). Sexton accuses her husband of babying their children, dishes clatter, noises rise and fall as the rage between Anne and Kayo finally subsides amid their daughters' pleas for them to leave one another alone. The traces from evenings like this appear in Linda's eyes. In order to locate the fear and anxiety that accrues there, one has to look beyond what is available to ordinary perception. One has to sustain an engagement with the image and what lies beyond it. One has to be willing to complicate what appears evident or straightforward.

"MY BELOVED, SIT UPON MY KNEE . . ."

What other narratives are housed in this publicity photograph? If you look closer, you will recognize the slight trace of a smile on Linda's face. Her subtle expression hints at the times when Sexton offered her children love and comfort in what Linda describes as the "proper proportion." In the following memory scene, it is late afternoon, and dusk settles in on this Thanksgiving day:

> Mother and I nestle beneath a thick wool afghan on top of the bed in Nana's bedroom. We are meant to be taking a nap, but, as usual, we are talking, sharing what we see and feel. Without knowing it, in this exchange of ideas and emotions Mother passes on to me her powers of observation; she shows me how to watch, how to see, how to record what transpires in the world around me. This is how I inherit her greatest gift. . . . The tree I have named the broccoli tree stands like a sentinel, silent and upright. It is not large, but it is sturdy and distinct. Mother's body curls around me in warm shelter. I am utterly cocooned. I am happy. Her fingers, long and lovely, trace a dance of tenderness

across my face. Feelings become memories; this memory becomes emblem-
atic, the truth of that particular day. (1994, 61)

Here, Sexton presents us with an emblem of the Winnicottian notion of
the "good-enough mother" who offers her child a "holding environment" that
keeps the body of the child and parent distinct, but close. In stark contrast to
the violent episodes between Sexton and Kayo that brought their daughters
to tears, this scene portrays Linda nested in an intimate milieu. Sexton passes
the time with Linda talking, actively observing, and recording the subtle details outside the bedroom window. Snuggling beneath a thick wool afghan, this
mother and daughter feel fully alive in the presence of one another.

The closeness that Linda remembers is not an isolated incident. Linda's
junior and high school years were decidedly different from earlier years, when
her mother was overwhelmed with the demands of her infants. As a teenager,
Linda would come home from school and often find Sexton on the phone, "her
legs propped high against the bookshelf in her writing room, tilted backward in
her desk chair, smoking" (98). Sexton would hang up and together they would
review the day. Linda recalls discussing poetry over tea as she and her mother
read Linda's drafts of poems. Linda knew full well that the sound of her mother's voice—its low throatiness combined with her fine sense of timing—could
easily "make a bad line sound like a good line." "She was gentle—kind, really,
with the lines that did not work, and never embarrassed me, even when I had
written something truly terrible" (97). Given the testimony offered by Sexton's
daughters, it appears that she had the capacity to provide them with a secure,
playful environment free from the weight of her depression and demands. As
her daughter Joy notes in my epigraph, what Sexton couldn't provide for her
children, she made sure they obtained from others.

ONE LOGIC OF FORGETTING

Nonetheless, as I review the materials documenting Sexton's relationship with
her daughters—letters exchanged, Linda's memoir, transcripts from Sexton's
psychiatric sessions with Dr. Orne—I find that my recurring concerns about
Sexton's place in the classroom press on. Even though there are indications that
Anne Sexton had the capacity to be a "good-enough mother," I continued to
be troubled by the question of whether she could be a "good-enough teacher."
Anne Sexton did not solely suffer with alcoholism and depression. When her
daughters were infants, she feared that she would kill them, and, during Linda's
adolescence, she made sexual use of her daughter's body. Linda recalls these
early mornings with terror and disgust:

> I remember seventh grade, my first year of junior high, when I had to get up
> earlier than either Joy or Daddy to catch my bus. That spring, Mother was not
> sleeping well, and she often crept into my room just as the sun came around
> the corner of my window. Sliding between the covers, she pressed her long

body against mine and I would wake to find her curled around me. Under the warm heap of covers, her naked belly and thighs pressed against my back and bare buttocks, my nightgown having bunched up around my waist during the night. As she rocked herself back and forth against me, her flesh damp and sticky, I closed my eyes and lay still, choking with disgust, my throat clenched against a scream I tamped down inside. I wanted to shove her away, but instead I waited for her to finish. The sound of that unvoiced scream echoes still inside my body. (1994, 107)

Linda can barely experience this trauma as it occurs as she "tamped down inside" and later, during an interview with Middlebrook, she recalls "waiting for something to be over. I don't think I wanted to know what it was" (1991, 223). Sexton's act of violence against her daughter is in fact a repetition of an earlier violent act Sexton's father, Ralph Harvey, committed against Anne when she was a child. Years later, Sexton reported this abuse to Dr. Martin Orne in therapy. Sexton also reported to Orne that she had been molested by her great-aunt, Anna Ladd Dingley ("Nana"). Was Anne Sexton's compulsion to repeat this event a perverse confrontation with a trauma that had imposed itself again and again? In *Beyond the Pleasure Principle*, Freud (1920) reminds us of the Greek meaning of the word *trauma*—wound, originally referring to an injury on the body. But in his text, he uses this word to refer to a wound inflicted on the mind—a breach in the mind's experience of time, self, and the world. Thus, trauma is not like a wound on the body, a physical and healable event. It is, as we learn from accounts of incestuous intrusions, a wound experienced too soon, too unexpectedly to be fully known. Trauma is therefore not available to consciousness until it imposes itself again, repeatedly, in the nightmares, flashbacks, and repetitive actions of the survivor (Daly, 1998).

The double-meaning of the word *trauma*—a wound to the mind or the body—raises difficult questions about the ways in which trauma impacts memory, forgetting, and the capacity to narrate traumatic experience. In her study of the emotional and rhetorical challenges that writers of autobiographical narratives face when they attempt to remember and organize traumatic experience, Leigh Gilmore (2001) turns to the work of psychologist Jennifer Freyd to consider the logic and function of an apparent forgetting. How does memory affect the narrative accounts of trauma? Freyd argues that the logic driving a child's pull to forget a traumatic event involving a parent is an adaptive response to the anguish and betrayal of losing a parent or caregiver. The parent kills him- or herself as a parent through the act of incest; the act of incest works, in fact, to create for the parent a place to hide from the child, leaving the child in the throes of a terrible, heartbreaking abandonment that is often resented more acutely than the abuse itself (Atwell-Vasey, 1998; Herman, 1992, 101).[1] The experience of trauma endured by the child is often accompanied by a loss or disruption of memory that Freyd refers to as a "motivated forgetting." The child is not only motivated to forget the event, but once the parent is lost through incest, a part of the child disappears as well. The loss of a secure and reliable holding environment coupled with the sexual intrusion of a parental figure generates a stigmatized identity in the child, blatantly provoking her to hide her "true self," for, in the words of psychoanalyst D. W. Winnicott, "the true self has been traumatized and it must never be found and wounded again" (1969, 33). To secure a sense of attachment with the abusive parent, the child persistently attempts to forget and be "good," becoming, as Judith Herman (1992) notes "a superb performer. . . . She may become an empathic caretaker for her parents, an efficient housekeeper, an academic achiever, a model of social conformity" (105). Or, as with Anne Sexton, the daughter may take on the role of the father's interlocutor with whom she addresses questions of identity, death, destruction, and creativity. In such cases, the daughter both identifies with the abusive parent and defies him or her. Whether the child becomes a superb performer or the parent's interlocutor, what remains difficult is the capacity to "feel real" (Winnicott, 1969).

In fact, the actions described combine to form a "false-self front" to cope with a painful and unpredictable world and to protect the "true self" that Winnicott associates with health and ingenuity. Thus, from the perspective of Winnicott, the true and false self exists within a field of concerns that must be negotiated within and against difficult emotions that include aggression, love, anxiety, loss, and fear. The use of a "false self front" to cope with the often inarticulate concerns provoked by incest offers the child a means through which to endure the loss of bodily integrity and the rupture in ordinary life, a rupture that defies the social conventions of bereavement, for cultural rituals provide little consolation for persons who have endured the trauma of incest and sexual abuse.

What significance is there in returning to Sexton's sexual abuse of her daughter, and to Ralph Harvey's alleged abuse of Anne Sexton, particularly in the context of a discussion about pedagogy, writing, and the work of reparation? Following the work of Britzman and Pitt, I believe that the qualities of trauma and the qualities of learning converge on an important point. Learning and trauma entail a breakdown of defenses, and, as Britzman and Pitt aptly describe it, "knowledge is felt as a force without being secured by meaning and understanding" (2004, 354). Learning bears a strong resemblance to trauma precisely because it provokes a crisis in meaning that often leaves a person feeling at a loss for words. Not only does a person feel inarticulate, but their sense of self, society, and meaning feel incoherent, and broken down. If, in fact, scholars such as Brenda Daly, Louise DeSalvo, Judith Herman, and Dawn Skorczewski are correct—that the trauma of incest obliterates cognitive frameworks for understanding the experience of abuse and, at the same time, can only be worked through through language, through narratives that are detailed, metaphoric, coherent, and that link events to emotional life—then writing has the potential to work as a powerful medium for repairing the effects of trauma.

Yet, the narrative forms available to tell of trauma are limited, and writing about trauma is particularly difficult, given that trauma is an experience, as noted by DeSalvo, "that essentially seems beyond language and form" (1999, 159). These rhetorical challenges make narratives of trauma vulnerable to doubt and resistant to conventional forms of expression. The narratives surrounding Sexton's history of incest illuminate these issues, for they raise questions about the stability and reliability of narratives that report a past history of traumatic injury. The doubt and disgust expressed by her doctors and critics exemplify a dynamic defense against knowledge that defies symbolization but at the same time calls out for remembering, for understanding, and for working through. Like Orne, I, too, am left doubting Sexton's accounts of incest. Did Sexton experience incest, or was her injury of another sort?

Gilmore turns to the work of Janice Haaken to consider why incest appears so pervasive in today's culture. In *Pillar of Salt,* Haaken (1998) argues that incest may be a metaphor for a range of causes of trauma. "Since there is some support for women to self-report as incest survivors," notes Haaken, "and because incest may resonate with a less definable experience of boundary violation, incest diagnoses have become prevalent" (26). For both Haaken and Gilmore, the important issue is that while these reports may tell a truth, they may not be rendering a literal truth. What women may be reaching for is a narrative that expresses an as yet undefined injury. Because incest narratives are culturally available and because sexual violence is the dominant lens through which women's trauma is viewed, these may be the only narrative terms made available to them to capture psychic traumas and physical abuse.

It appears that both Middlebrook and Orne understood Sexton's reports of her father's sexual abuse along the lines of reasoning outlined by Haaken. Middlebook's conclusions are measured. "For Sexton the artist," Middlebrook writes, "the developmentally layered and conflicted love of a girl for her father was a source of insight into the psychological and social complexity of living as a woman . . . [the veracity of the incest narrative cannot be established historically, but that does not mean that it didn't, in a profound and lasting sense, 'happen']" (1991, 58). Here, Middlebrook echoes the insights set forth by Haaken—that the key to attending to narratives of incest lies in not literalizing the report, but in recognizing that for women, sexual storytelling is a complex process that necessarily and appropriately combines fantasy with memory as it develops over time in therapy (Gilmore, 2001, 26). Such narratives work toward capturing, as noted earlier, an as yet unnamed injury that has not been made available to the narrative structures that culture and society deem worthy of articulation (Gilmore, 2001). The suspicion of and resistance to believe narratives of trauma is evident in a letter that Sexton's nieces, Lisa Taylor Tompson and Mary Gray Ford, wrote to the *New York Times* soon after Middlebrook's biography was published in 1991.

> Aside from some very serious ethical and moral issues, we find it especially saddening that Anne's remarks, made in some sort of hypnotic trance, are treated as statements of truth rather than what they are—the perceptions

of a seriously troubled woman who saw ominous undertones in every kind word, and peril in the most innocent remark. . . . We don't know what made Anne the way she was, and never will. . . . All of the speculation in the world, including the wild speculation and completely unwarranted conclusions in Diane Wood Middlebrook's book, won't answer the question. But one thing is certain: this puerile, psychobabble attempt to explain the roots of Anne Sexton's poetic creativity does a severe disservice to people who never did her a moment's harm by thought, word, or deed. . . . Her great-aunt Nana—a woman then in her 80's—may have given Anne a back rub, but it is patently ridiculous to suggest that she did so with salacious intent. . . . Similarly, our grandfather Ralph Harvey most certainly did not abuse Anne, sexually or otherwise."[2]

How reliable can a woman who suffered with mental illness be? Dr. Martin Orne casts doubt on Sexton's claims as well.

"I dealt with it in therapy as a real event," he told Middlebrook, "because there were times that it was real to her. . . . If you ask me either as a psychiatrist or as a scientist, however, I would have to say I am virtually certain that it never occurred. It's not plausible the way she described it, and it wasn't the father's style when he was drinking. But it fit her feelings about her father having abused her, and since she sexualized everything, it would become the metaphor with which [she'd] deal with it."[3]

Orne's line, "It would become the metaphor with which [she'd] deal with it" points to the difficult-to-define experience of bodily boundary violation that Haaken addresses in her studies. There was no question that Ralph Harvey was intrusive and sexually hostile toward his daughter, and he used his sexual hostility to cling to her when she dated boys. Sexton's psychiatric tapes include memories of her father spanking her with his riding crop, and calling her a "little bitch." It is clear from Sexton's memory, as well as from her mother's, that her father frequently launched verbally aggressive insults against her as she moved into adolescence. He often verbally attacked her at the dinner table, scrutinized her acne, made sounds and motions of disgust, refused to look at her, and would then criticize her and withdraw from her and the family. Sexton's father also spoke viciously behind her back. One evening, as she was leaving the house on a date, he remarked to Sexton's mother, "It looks like she's going out to get fucked" (Middlebrook, 1991, 57). In her detailed analysis of Sexton's treatment by Dr. Orne, Susan Kavaler-Adler (2000) maintains that Sexton's father was overly involved with his daughter in ways that suggest intrusive, incestuous, and erotically aggressive behavior. These actions, argues Kavaler-Adler, point to a dire and destructive form of psychic intrusion.[4]

Why is Sexton's memory of incest doubted by her psychiatrist and her biographer? Memory must be submitted to tests, and, memory can, as we know, only possess the degree of authority held by the person who remembers. This is what is intended by Foucault's phrase "a politics of memory." A politics of persons and their actions operates, as Foucault (1975) theorizes, in a social and psychic field of power. Those who possess sanctioned authority are believed, while those who do not possess such authority are not. This psychic field of power is informed by the events that have been forgotten, encrypted, and repressed. Lapses in memory associated with trauma have a history as well. They can be traced to controversies about the study of memory, and debates about "false memory," all of which are instances of battles forged over truth telling, identity, and whose word possesses the weight of "truth" and "verifiability." First-person accounts of trauma by women have always been doubted when they put forward accounts of sexual trauma because women's ways of representing themselves challenge the narrative accounts made by the dominant representative person. The dominant representative person, as explained by Gilmore, works like this:

> If you are an autobiographer, then you stand in the place of the representative person. Your position there enables the kind of identification that characterizes autobiography. If you act, then, as the mirror of the self (for me), then in my identification with you I substitute myself for you, the other. If I am barred from doing that by your non-representativeness, I withdraw my identification, and, quite likely, the sympathy that flows from it. (2001, 22)

Gilmore argues that trauma narratives composed by women and minority men and women more often than not provoke skepticism in readers, precisely because they make evident the tension between identification and representation and they pressure the reader to assume a position of masochism or voyeurism (22). "The reader," as Gilmore astutely points out, " is invited to find himself or herself in the figure of the representative, or to enjoy a kind of pleasure in the narrative organization of pain, in the case of trauma accounts" (22). In short, the autobiographies written by marginalized people are less likely to be believed because of the conflicts with other predominant figures.

Drawing on limit cases of autobiography such as Dorothy Allison's *Bastard Out of Carolina* and Jamaica Kincaid's *The Autobiography of My Mother*, Gilmore proposes that autobiography, which performs at the margins of fiction and autobiography, works to maneuver out of the traps of identification, voyeurism, and surveillance. These writers use rhetorical tactics to invite and resist identification—avoiding the conventional constraints imposed by the autobiographical *I* (2001, 22–23). Perhaps Sexton made use of incest narratives in therapy because they were the only narratives available that could approximate the more subtle, yet as yet unnamed experiences of trauma she struggled with. As a writer and teacher, however, she worked to articulate a more expansive form of personal narrative, one that stressed, albeit intuitively, that language is a medium through which the self is at once composed and decentered. The remark that Sexton makes to her students, "I am often being personal, but I'm not being personal about myself," suggests an alternative composition for life writing about trauma—one that expands the notion of "truth" as conceived by traditions of "confessional" writing, to the "borderland" between personal writing, creative nonfiction, and fiction (Gilmore, 2001, 49). What is present in Sexton's writing that is not quite fiction, but a bit like nonfiction, not quite autobiography, but somewhat like it? How should this work be read? What lessons does Sexton disclose to her students about the use of "truth" and "fact" when describing their experiences (63)?

The *I* that Sexton elaborates on in her teaching documents can be read, not simply as an expression of personal suffering, as suggested by so many of her critics, but also as an expression of the ways in which personal suffering absorbs and is attached to social life. This is evident in the assignments that Sexton designed for her students, particularly in the following exercise, in which she refers to an uncollected poem she wrote soon after Robert Kennedy's assassination.

> It is quite intriguing to me to become another person. I remember when Robert Kennedy was killed, another death, another assassination. Despite the sorrow I felt there was something else stirring, an image, a personality, a psyche, a need to kill. The man as assassin. What was his emotion as he looked through the gun sight and captured that face, that chest, that mouth, quick and alive, waiting for murder? What I wrote was very imagistic, and perhaps surreal, but how feverish that moment. How surreal it would be. [5]

Sexton goes on to tell her students that she felt this poem was rejected by the *New Yorker* because it was written too soon after Kennedy's assassination. Perhaps, she notes, "it upset them, and they were afraid of public reaction: anger, distaste, a kind of revulsion on the part of the reader that could take such an immediate view which now we see historically and look into the villain's heart and speak for him."[6] What can be learned from looking into the villain's heart? Sexton's use of personae can be understood as a means for bringing her students into closer contact with aspects of themselves that, while deeply intimate, remain radically unknown to them. Such intimate disturbances can never be severed or successfully denied, for they return at the most unsuspected moments, taking us off guard, bringing us face to face with forbidden lost loves or aspects of our selves that we fear and thus find far too disturbing to address (Britzman, 1998; Bronfen, 1998, 305; Taubman, 2006). Thus, the foreign and the familiar intermingle, resisting control and easy categorizations.

MOVING TOWARD REPARATION

The role that memory plays in writing about trauma and the rhetorical challenges posed to the writer of such accounts raise a related, more sensitive challenge: How can a person who composes a narrative of trauma speak of love in the midst of so much pain? (Allison, 1992; Gilmore, 2001, 47).

This is precisely the subtext of Linda Gray Sexton's memoir. As her mother's daughter and appointed protector, in life and death (Linda is the literary executor of her mother's estate), Linda Gray Sexton writes in order to "seize hold of our relationship . . . as I run to and from my mother, to and from my-self" (1994, 10). Her narrative offers a vivid portrait of how traumatic histories haunt and hurt, and how trauma casts people into exile from their homes and those they love, stealing their capacity to risk love again. While Linda Gray Sexton writes clearly of her mother's sexual abuse of her body, Middlebrook is more speculative. She suggests that Sexton may have been disassociated when abusing Linda. Middlebrook writes:

> Sexton never acknowledged to her daughter that she was conscious of trans-gression, but how could she have failed to see how wrong this was? The most generous interpretation is that she may have been very dissociated when she made sexual use of Linda. Sexton identified deeply with this daughter, through whom she relived her own psychological development. . . . Linda concurs with this view of her behavior; as she put it later, "the compulsion to repeat and to recast her own history was just too strong." Sexton turned to Linda whenever she was feeling particularly fragile, and Linda bore this as one of the costs of her mother's instability. (1991, 223–224)

What is called for in the presence of narratives of trauma—compassion, anger, rage? Is the harm done to Linda minimized if Sexton actually was disas-sociated during these abusive episodes? Did the strain of caution in Middle-brook's account, and her desire for a causal, compassionate explanation, cast Linda's experience of incest into the realm of disavowed traumas that cannot be mourned precisely because the impact of their horror cannot be fully ar-ticulated in public? The maternal body of Anne Sexton presents her daughter with the terrifying and most loving of situations. From her, Linda learns the possibilities and constraints attached to whom she may become. And from her mother, Linda inherits the memories of intolerable abuse that cannot be fully remembered or forgotten, until years later, after experiencing childbirth, raising children, breaking down emotionally and physically, and then writing about it. Through writing, Linda learned how *not* to die with her mother, thereby ex-tending her mother's most powerful lesson—that writing can potentially save one's life.

And then there is Anne Sexton's psychic predicament—her failure to be, in Winnicott's terms, a good-enough mother. By failing to fulfill this role, she was considered a failure. Is it significant that this failure was associated with an inherited melancholic strain, a loss that was attached to shameful acts of incest and intensified by the stereotypical demands that post–World War II America placed on middle-class women? These demands often thrust women into states described by Michael Eigen as the "lost-I feeling" (1993). This feeling that Eigen strives to capture depicts how a person can feel so intruded upon and unable to breath, so lost to the desires of others, that their sense of self hardens and contracts to the point of insensibility. Left with an impoverished sense of being, this sense of loss sabotages the trusted boundaries between self and other and poses specific threats to the project of "self-representation." How can a writer represent a self, if that self is vulnerable to feeling shamed, impoverished, or threatened?

To what extent do the demands placed on the maternal figure to be good enough ironically leave her vulnerable to sliding into a "false self" in order to provide her child with the proper holding environment? Winnicott's postwar writings are fraught with a subtle ambivalence about how active the subjectivity of the mother should be with respect to her child's ruthless love—and her need to make repeated and absolute claims upon her. While the good-enough mother must be available to her child, she must not be too satiating, otherwise the child's "developing self" will be obstructed (Kavaler-Adler, 2000, 62). In the event that the mother is incapable of meeting the child's needs, the mother must learn to "act as if" she is good enough, masquerading, if you will, so as to provide her child with what is necessary for her development. Thus, we bump up against another paradox in the work of Winnicott. While, on the one hand, a mother must be genuine, personal, confident, and spontaneous, on the other hand, if she is depressed, anxious, or preoccupied, she must not be genuine in the presence of the child *who is too anxious or fearful to bear the presence of the mother's difficult subjectivities* (Phillips, 1988, 67).

Winnicott (1965) is steady in his belief that if the maternal figure fails to withstand her child's "imperial claims" and impinges her will on her child, then the child is inclined to adapt by resorting to compliance, which in turn creates a lost sense of "aliveness" and "feeling real." These terms exceed the idea of simply existing. They call for a particular capacity to exist as oneself, and to have a self to, as Phillips explains, "retreat to for relaxation" (1989, 128). The absolute patience, sense of attunement, and sustained resilience necessary to be good enough, so as to provide the child with the strength to pursue her curiosities stands as quite remarkable, ideal really. And while Winnicott's concept of good-enough mothering is compelling, I fear that it demands from the maternal figure a set of serious compromises that affects her capacity for cultivating her own curiosities and interests. Before turning to Sexton's early years as a mother, I have some concerns with Winnicott's claims, particularly with the question of what it means to be a subject, particularly a subject of desire, as it has important implications for understanding the impact that authority and agency has for female teachers and the teaching life of Anne Sexton. I turn to Anne Sexton's struggles as a mother and teacher in order to consider the implications of what it means when "maternal work" is so essential, not only to the constitution of the developing mind of the child, but to the psychic strength of a nation. These implications are particularly important to attend to given that female subjectivity is so rarely represented in maternal and educational discourses as active and desirous. Moreover, the theory Winnicott develops with respect to cultivating a "true self" in the presence of a social field that barely tolerates the sexual and intellectual appetites of women raises important questions about what it means to represent a self, both in writing and in the classroom, when that self is inclined to hide so as not to be vulnerable to shame, scrutiny, or humiliation.

CONCERNS WITH WINNICOTT'S IDEAS

Winnicott shows little regard for the difficult subjectivities of the mother. In fact, Winnicott insists that in instances when the mother must disillusion her child by turning to her own work and interests, the good-enough mother must do so in the name of the infant, not in the name of her own curiosities or needs. The mother who is inattentive, particularly at the beginning of an infant's life, was, in Winnicott's view, a "saboteur" of the child's developmental process—moving dangerously close to impinging on the continuity of care that was so crucial in creating a sense of well-being for the baby. Adam Phillips confirms the assessment of Winnicott's disregard for the subjectivity of the mother in the following passage: "Though not blaming mothers for their 'failures,' he was implicitly demanding everything of them at the very beginning. 'Only if a mother is sensitized in the way I am describing,' he writes with unusually dogmatic conviction, 'can she feel herself into her infant's place and so meet the infant's needs'" (122).

The sensitized position required of the good-enough mother cannot account for the ruptures and sorrow that emerge in the life of the mother—nor do these theories offer places for transgression or renewal outside of platitudes of exercising compassion for Others or attuning to the child's needs. The concerns I raise here resonate with the recent scholarship of Alice Pitt. In her analysis of the place of the mother in psychoanalytic studies, literary and educational theory, Pitt (2006) also turns to Winnicott's concept of the good-enough mother to ask why "the mother must be destroyed and what remains after such a terrifying act." Pitt addresses not only the lack of regard that Winnicott shows for the subjectivities of the mother, but the contingency he establishes in his work between becoming a "speaking subject" of our own histories and destroying the mother—body, breast, and subjectivity. Pitt's close readings of Winnicott advance the argument that while he placed the maternal figure at the center of his psychoanalytic theory, he did so solely for the purpose of raising good-enough children. Paradoxically, he made it necessary for the child to aggressively devour the mother so that the child can in turn claim the status of a speaking subject who has the capacity to engage her interests and curiosities—to *use* the world rather than solely *relate* to it. Again, keeping our attention on the mother, in order for the child to symbolize, she must be capable of symbolizing the loss of the mother (a lost reality—hence, making symbol formation contingent on a fantasy of the mother's destruction). What is less often attended to is the psychic and existential impact this destruction brings about for women and their children (2006, 21).

We can hear the anxiety of mothers forsaking their appetites in the personae who circulate throughout Sexton's poetry. In her poem, "Two Sons," the persona of the mother has grown "old on her bitterness," abandoned by her sons who have married.

> Both of you monopolized
> with no real forwarding address
> except for two silly postcards you bothered to send home,
> one of them written in grease
> as you undid her dress

What emerges from these lines are disturbing images of an abandoned, intrusive, and bitter mother. But there is more. One has to wonder if Sexton was mimicking the maternal ideal here—offering her readers a double vision that disrupts the selfless, ever-gracious portrait of the good-enough mother, warning her readers of the bitterness that festers when appetites are harnessed and one is asked to live alienated from desire. While her boys are, as the narrator suggests, "made of my cooking, those suppers of starch and beef, and with my library, my medicine, my bath water," they grow as they should and move on. The discourse of mimicry expresses not only what is known and permitted, but also what is known but must be kept concealed; it is in this sense that mimicry is a discourse that is uttered between the lines, both against the rules and within them (Bhaba, 1994, 88). Lacan (1978, 99) describes mimicry as camouflage that refuses to harmonize the repression of difference. While the figure in this poem appears as mother, her status as a "jilted nurturer" produces a menacing taste that raises questions about what aspects of her self the maternal figure must abandon, and what aspects of the maternal her children are required to destroy in order to *use* the world. These questions are not addressed explicitly by Winnicott, but they can be explored between the lines of Sexton's poetry and within the narratives that shape her life as a mother and a teacher.

EXCESSES OF PASSION AND CONFLICT IN NARRATIVES OF TRAUMA

In an interview with Barbara Kevles in 1972, Sexton describes the first attempt to end her life as a departure from the middle-class conventions of the time:

> Until I was twenty-eight I had a kind of buried self who didn't know she could do anything but make white sauce and diaper babies. I didn't know I had any creative depths. I was a victim of the American Dream, the bourgeois, middle-class dream. All I wanted was a little piece of life, to be married, to have children. I thought the nightmares, the visions; the demons would go away if there were enough love to put them down. I was trying my damnedest to lead a conventional life, for that was how I was brought up, and it was what my husband wanted of me. But one can't build little white picket fences to keep nightmares out. The surface cracked when I was about twenty-eight. I had a psychotic break and tried to kill myself. (84)

What do these nightmares contain? This retrospective account of the reasons behind her first suicide attempt invokes one of her signature images—the cracked surface of a conventional, bourgeois dream shattered by the emergence of a self that had been submerged in a belief in love. What kind of love was Sexton referring to in this statement? Idealized maternal love comes to mind—embedded in the stifling social situation that existed for women at the time. "All I wanted was ... to be married, to have children.... I thought the ... demons would go away if there were enough love to put them down." In her description of struggle, Sexton introduces us to a bourgeois domestic space, a site, if you will, for demonic invasions that crack and displace her from home and family. The unhomely moments portrayed by Sexton in her poetry relate her traumatic personal, psychic history to a wider political existence. Sexton, molested by her own father, relays a belated repetition of the violent history of women at the hands of their fathers' power, fear and desire to kill themselves off as fathers. Sexton does not hide from sight her father's sexual use of her body. By making this moment visible as one among many of the demonic visions that are rendered in her poetry, in therapy, and more subtly in her teaching, she specifies the patriarchal, gendered nature of civil society. Sexton provokes us to consider the ways in which we might direct our pedagogy toward what we cannot bear to know, asking us to create an inconsolable memory in the face of the violence of incest. We would then conceptualize incest as a profound form of domestic colonization that begins at home and naturalizes the invasions of psyches, consciousness, bodies, and nations. The father is oppressor; just and unjust, moderate and rapacious, vigorous and despotic; these instances of contradictory belief raise questions about the act of incest, an act of violence that happens between the lines and borders of identity itself, between parent and child, siblings, intermingling and contaminating blood lines and genealogical lines, erasing difference, and, in the extreme, erupting into the degeneration of family and narrative.

Sexton confessed to "feeling real," in the world of poets and in the classroom. Her feelings are recorded in the teaching journals she kept for Herbert Kohl while working with the Teachers and Writers Collaborative in 1967. "When I give a reading, I feel that I'm faking it, and when I'm in class, I'm not faking it. No ... not any more," she wrote. The self that emerges after Sexton's "psychotic break," would be described by Winnicott as her "true self," for it offered her the opportunity to feel alive, to experience spontaneity and to begin to be free from the demands of authoritative figures. Sexton often described writing poetry as a movement through death to a new life, "Inherent in the process is a rebirth of a sense of self, each time stripping away a dead self" (1974, 86).

Between having children, writing, and teaching, however, Sexton broke. Despite stretches of confidence and remarkable achievements, her psyche became more and more fragile. As Sexton notes in her retrospective account to Barbara Kevles, motherhood and marriage provoked her to feel torn up, anxious, and lonely. In 1955, she began to feel the intensifying pain of her deepening breakdown, as she no longer was able to care for her children, to cook, or to feel any sense of direction. In a handwritten note to Dr. Orne early that winter, after more than a year of treatment, she writes:

> I am so alone—nothing seems worth while I walk from room to room trying to think of something to do—for a while I will do something, make cookies or clean the bathroom—make beds—answer the telephone—but all along I have this almost terrible energy in me and nothing seems to help. . . . I sit in a chair and try to read a magazine and I twirl my hair until it is a mass [of] snarls—then as I pass a mirror I see myself and comb it again. Then I walk up and down the room—back and forth—and I feel like a caged tiger. . . . Now Kayo is gone—his absence absolutely removes all reason to begin or end. I am rudderless with no direction. . . . My sexual life is in reality a hideous mess and I don't understand it and furthermore I don't want to discuss it or understand it. . . . Here I am so oversexed that I have to struggle not to masturbate most of the day—and I certainly don't want to discus that—but it's true neverthe-less—and when Kayo starts to make love to me I can't concentrate on it—
>
> I had Joy for the weekend and she has gone back today—I love her, she is adorable and winning—but seems to take so much patience and energy and I was glad to see her go. I guess I don't love anyone—that is a terrible statement and now I am crying. . . . My heart pounds and it's all I can hear—my feeling for my children does not surpass my desire to be free of their demands upon my emotions. What have I got? Who would want to live feeling that way? (qtd. in Middlebrook, 1991, 36–37)

Sexton's daughters were young at this time, and she had barely been capable of caring for them. Soon after giving birth to Joy in August 1955, she began to experience serious episodes of depression and developed a fear of being alone with her babies. She could not withstand the acute demands of her infants. Sexton began to feel intense rage at Linda; she would grab her and begin slapping and choking her. Fearful that she would kill her children, she turned to her extended family, who offered practical help—housekeeping, payment of medical bills, and company while her husband was away on business trips.

Only in her poetry did she display understanding of the infant's needs. In one of her most well-known poems, "Unknown Girl in the Maternity Ward," she wrote:

> Child, the current of your breath is six days long.
> You lie, a small knuckle on my white bed;
> lie, fisted like a snail, so small and strong
> at my breast. Your lips are animals; you are fed
> with love. At first hunger is not wrong.

Unlike the poet who wrote this poem, the narrator understands the early hungers of the infant, their ruthless love and desire for constant sustenance. This poem is in fact part of a larger recurring pattern in which Sexton performs a precarious inversion of a psychic anguish that she can no longer contain after the birth of her daughters.

After a close call with suicide in 1955, Sexton was hospitalized at Westwood Lodge, where, notes Middlebrook (1991), in 1950, Dr. Brunner-Orne, Martin Orne's mother, had treated Sexton's father for alcoholism, and where, sometime earlier, she had treated his sister, Francis for the same problem (33). Eventually, Sexton's mother-in-law Billie cared for her daughters.

Middlebrook notes that the painful sense of bewilderment haunting Sexton was certainly justifiable, for there were no apparent answers to the roots of her misery. "Her history and her symptoms," posits Middlebrook, "put her in ambiguous diagnostic territory that is only somewhat clearer today than it was in 1956. Whatever the constitutional givens, Sexton's difficulties obviously had much to do with the psychological dynamics into which motherhood thrust her" (37). With each breakdown, Sexton had to endure the loss of a familiar geography, returning again and again to the psychiatric wing of Massachusetts General Hospital or Westwood Lodge. These hospitalizations induced extreme experiences of psychic lability, while at the same time offered her a strange sense of comfort. It was difficult for Sexton to withstand a change in geography, for leaving town, leaving the house, or traveling to give a poetry reading could paralyze her. Thus, while she suffered with a sense of "too much home" that could leave her feeling engulfed by domestic space, Sexton also felt alien in her own skin, displaced and longing for home. Suffering with acute agoraphobia throughout her adult life, she felt far too vulnerable to leave the house or to travel unless she was in the company of trusted companions, and she drank heavily to ease her anxieties before performing in public (Middlebrook, 1991, 127–128).

Sexton began her therapeutic sessions with Dr. Martin Orne in 1956. Their work ushered her into the writing workshops with poet John Holmes and offered her a "potential space" that cultivated within her the stunning sensation of "feeling real."

The Writing Workshop

By 1960, it had been four years since Sexton's first hospitalization. She continued to grow as a writer, to forge important and lasting relationships with fellow poets, and to attend bi-monthly workshops with her colleagues in the living room of John Holmes. Holmes had established the signature method through which poets critiqued one another's work, and sought out from one another, as Robert Creeley once noted "water to drink". The tradition of the workshop was long and is eloquently documented by Holmes in a chapter entitled "Biographies of Five Poems" in his book, *Writing Poetry*. In this collection, Holmes praises the workshop as a form of artistic collaboration, particularly the workshops he attended in the 1940s with John Ciardi, Richard Eberhart, May Sarton, and Richard Wilbur. Holmes openly discussed with his readers how his poems evolved through multiple drafts, from first notes to finished form. For Sexton, who never attended college or formally studied literature, the workshops she participated in with John Holmes were akin to a prestigious tutorial. Poets gathered to present works-in-progress, to draft out lines, to listen for the half-spoken image, and to engage, recalls George Starbuck, in wordplay (Middlebrook, 1991, 97–101).

> Sexton gravitated toward generating images, exploring the emotional life and working toward releasing conventional response. She often described how the creative impulse contributed, in significant ways, to challenging her desire for oblivion. Even when Sexton fell into the deepest of depressions, she remained grateful to the power of poetry to "exorcise her death wishes," a phrase given to her by Maxine Kumin and from which she derived comfort. In a letter to Anne Clarke, a psychiatrist, close friend, and one-time lover whom Tillie Olsen introduced Sexton to while they were fellows at the Bunting Institute, Sexton discusses the plans she has for her collection of poems, *The Death Notebooks*. She speculates that she may call one section "The Wood of the Suicides," after Dante's *Inferno*—"I am fascinated with the whole thing and as I work on it I create it (instead of doing it) . . . a fine substitute!" (1977, 232)

Kumin describes her approach to workshopping as "never meek":

> It was awesome the way she could arrive at our bi-monthly sessions with three, four, even five new and complicated poems . . . she . . . respected the counsel of others. She gave generous help to her colleagues, and she required, demanded, insisted on generous response. As a result of this experience, Anne came to believe in the value of the workshop. She loved growing in this way, and she urged the method on her students at Boston University, Colgate, Oberlin and in other workshops she conducted from time to time. (1981, xxv)

Sexton recognized the restorative potential in writing, and she spoke explicitly about the ways in which writing saved her life, how writing gave her life order, and, at times, a sense of composure. In her notes for the seventh lecture she gave at Colgate University she wrote:

> As I have said elsewhere, a formal structure works as a kind of superego. You say to yourself, "This is an impossible form. I could not even write a sentence to fit it, much less a poem." So you put your mind to that problem. You are inhibited because the form and therefore your unconscious can have its way. Nothing inhibits it, and it is allowed to have free rein to tell its story. I once said that form was a cage, and if you had a good strong cage, you could let some really wild animals in it. Thus, the wild animals are the content and the cage is the form.[7]

The structure of the writing workshops Sexton attended offered her access to a collaborative and social milieu that enabled her to repair the profound sense of loss, anxiety, isolation, and displacement she felt as a mother, daughter, and wife in post–World War II America. However, these workshops Sexton conducted with her students *did not* create a congenial milieu in which she could perform as a "good-enough teacher." Rather, the workshops she led at Boston and Colgate Universities can be read as exemplary of how Sexton used pedagogical and narrative tactics to represent female experiences that *exceeded* the limits of the "good-enough mother." The writing exercises that Sexton used in her workshops illuminate the constraints inherent in the ideal of the "good-enough mother/teacher" as well as the "tricks" or "pedagogical tactics" available for comprehensively transgressing the limits of these images. This work exceeds the role of "good-enough" mothering and teaching because it actively engages the aspects of female subjectivity that are difficult to articulate. Sexton believed, recalls Maxine Kumin, "that the hardest truths would come to light if they were made to fit a stanzaic pattern, a rhyme scheme, a prevailing meter" (1981, xxv). Indeed, Sexton was fearless in her study of the vicissitudes between love and hate and her inquiry into the love that both hurts and comforts us.

The work of understanding reparation as an act that is both reflective and imaginative has been described by Rinaldo Walcott (1998) and Ursula A. Kelly (2004) as a radical form of pedagogical consciousness. Neither Walcott nor Kelly romanticize such a project. They fully understand that much harm has been taken up by educators in the name of good intentions. What urges each of them on is the possibility for using Melanie Klein's work to illuminate a pedagogy that productively addresses defeat and trauma as more than loss. A pedagogy of reparation calls on educators to study our problematic attachments, as well as to consider how the loves in our lives have both helped and hindered us, cared for and hurt us (Kelly, 2004, 165–166; Walcott, 2005). One place such work might begin is to address the simultaneous presence of irreconcilables— the daughter's love for the mother who cannot care for her; the daughter's attachment to a rapacious, cruel father. Sexton combines self-representation, fiction, fairytales, poetry, and plays to create a means through which to love her shameful and shamed family, for throughout the story of Anne Sexton and her daughter Linda, love persists, even in the midst of rage, even as it allows for harm, even as it opens the front door of the house on 12 Clearwater Drive, where violence enters over cocktails and calls it "home" (Gilmore, 2001, 66).

In the following section, I present two exercises that Sexton devised for the workshops she taught at Boston and Colgate Universities. In each instance, she speaks to her students about the emotions that lie beneath grief—sorrow, feelings of guilt and forgiveness—as she refrains from preoccupations with injury and victimization. As Sexton speaks about her composing process to her students, she contemplates the objects of her displacement, clearly scrutinizing what she refers to as the "leftovers of a life" among the inheritance of objects—"the suites, the cars, the scrapbook"—for what they can tell her of how love both taught and hurt her (Gilmore, 2001). Her pedagogical tactics, like many of the lines in her writing, offer a kind of serious playfulness where studies of *our* Otherness can unfold.

Teaching as Reparation

By 1969, the year Sexton began teaching at Boston University, she had accrued some important experiences in the seminar room. Prior to her appointment at Boston University, Sexton had taught a seminar at Radcliffe College, enjoyed the numerous post-reading visits at college campuses, and had participated in a nationwide program with Herbert Kohl and the Teachers and Writers Collaborative. Teachers and Writers was composed of an eclectic group of people including Jonathan Kozol, Richard Lewis, Ishmael Reed, June Jordan, Muriel Rukeyser, and Grace Paley. Through her affiliation with Teachers and Writers, Sexton co-taught English at Wayland High School in Wayland, Massachusetts, with Robert Clawson. By September 1972, Sexton had successfully negotiated a position with Boston University. She was appointed a half-time professor with a salary of $10,000 for a semester's work and a five-year contract—quite an accomplishment for a female instructor teaching in the academy at the time.

Sexton drew a good deal on the pedagogical approach taken by John Holmes in her writing workshops, often informing her students on the first day of class that they will learn "how badly a poem can begin," and then, through revision, and a series of what she referred to as her "tricks," how her drafts evolved into a complete poem. In fact, as I read through Sexton's discussions with her students, I felt she practically imitated Holmes word for word. In a 1972 workshop she gave at Colgate University, Sexton presents her students with a set of her manuscripts for her poem, "All My Pretty Ones."

> I have on my desk 6 pages of what is called beginning worksheets of "All My Pretty Ones." I thought I'd kind of read you parts from each page so you might see, line by line, how very badly it began, how it almost never got written. We will play detective. We're going to see how a poem is made and remade and remade. I purposefully have not re-read these. What they will show you of my personal life I have no idea. It is a very vulnerable position to show your worksheets, but I felt it would greatly enhance your knowledge of me as well as show you how badly a poem can begin and then how it can be rescued. We will play detective together. We will look at the beginnings, the early fumblings, the jottings and find clues. I want you to look as hard as I will look. . . . I began badly, with raw emotion and bitterness, with no good lines, no form nothing but the need to give reality to feelings. . . . I'll give it to you rough as it was.[8]

Apparently, a poem, like a life, can start out badly. But there are rhetorical tactics a person can draw on to "rescue" bitterness and bad lines from demise—to repair a poem, so to speak, to make it good. Sexton moves her narrative forward by filling her students in on the significance of the list of the objects she includes.

> *All My Pretty Ones* tells the story of an inheritance of objects, the suits, the cars, the pictures, the scrapbook, my mother's diary. . . . We have the leftovers of a life, the gifts I did not choose, a gold key, half of a woolen mill, twenty

suits, an English Ford, boxes of pictures, and my mother's diary in which she
wrote of my father. I'm not sure of the time lapses, probably these five pages
took me over a week of attempts.[9]

There are traces of ambivalence threaded through this pedagogical scene,
for Sexton's inheritance is both contained and exceeded by the limits of this list.
Embodied in each object are memories of hate, guilt, and love. What Sexton
doesn't include in this workshop discussion, but renders in her poem, are a series
of facts. The golden key refers to the residence her father could no longer afford,
many of the pictures were of people "I do not know. I touched their cardboard
faces. They must go." The diary contains all that her mother "does not say" of her
father's "alcoholic tendency." Perhaps one reason I find this poem compelling is
because *All My Pretty Ones* works to redirect the guilt, destruction, and sense of
abandonment felt in this family to the question of forgiveness and of love. The
final lines of the published poem read like this:

Only in this hoarded span will love persevere.
Whether you are pretty or not, I outlive you,
bend down my strange face to yours and forgive you.

Not only does Sexton speak to her students of what and who has been
destroyed, but she moves through an arch of emotion, thereby displacing her
anger with forgiveness, and making it possible to love again. This love takes
hold in the face of difference, separation, and the fear that one's lineage can seep
into one's psyche uninvited. "My God, father, each Christmas Day with your
blood, will I drink down your glass of wine."

Here, the analogy between Anne Sexton's performance as a teacher and
the psychic dilemmas she struggled with as a daughter and a mother become
especially vivid. The exercises to which she introduced her students in writing workshops engaged them in claiming or giving voice to alterity. In other
words, Sexton asserted her difference from the assigned role of the "good-
enough mother," by drawing on her concerns rather than displacing them, and
by disrupting and interfering in her students' taken-for-granted notions about
what forms of personae offer educative possibilities. Included among Sexton's
central concerns is a study of problematic attachments—to family, lovers, and
addictions. Lacan used the term *extimacy* to suggest that "the most intimate
is at the same time the most hidden ... the most intimate is not a point of
transparency, but rather a point of opacity. ... Extimacy says that the intimate is
Other—like a foreign body, a parasite (Bronfen, 1998, 31; Jacques-Alain Miller,
1988, 123). Lacan's notion of extimacy is useful for discussing Sexton's teaching
because it designates the encrypted presence of kernels of traumatic knowledge
housed in the symbolic register where repressed material returns. Sexton hoped
her workshops would revive a sense of the uncanny, and self-estrangement, as
made evident in the following questions she poses to her students at Colgate
University:

Now, if I'm not a cripple, how can I write a poem about being one? In what ways am I a cripple still? How did I come to writing about myself? How did I come to be a confessional poet who vomits up her past every ugly detail onto the page? I started to write about myself because it was something I knew well. Beyond this is the need to confess and admit one's guilt and be forgiven. With every poem it is as if I were on trial, pleading my case before the court of angels and hoping for a pardon. And now, I'm going to give you an in-class assignment: Write a short poem or character sketch using a persona. Suggestions: the wife beater from the point of view of the man who beats his wife telling something of his psyche or the wife who is beaten telling something of her psyche. Why in each case do they stay together? What imagery is called up by their different attitudes? Become that person. Put on that mask. Or . . . find a persona poem and explain what techniques are used to convince you that this is authentic. Verify with examples from the poem. Write out in prose the story being told. Examples of persona poems are Keats "Crazy Jane"; Browning's "My Last Duchess," in books by Randal Jarrell you ought to find a female persona. John Crow Ransom's *Piazza Piece,* or to get a little more contemporary, and perhaps interesting, Ted Hughes . . . lots of persona.[10]

When Melanie Klein writes that "a good relation to ourselves is a condition for tolerance and wisdom toward others" (1961, 342), and that this ability to love has developed from those who meant much to us in the past, even if they have betrayed us, she is calling on us to learn to live within the tension of opposites—within the tension of love and hate, of innocence and guilt. Sexton's question, "In what ways am I a cripple still?" opens up the possibility to imagine a tangle of belonging and not belonging, vulnerability and strength, losing and finding again the lost object of love. The poem this question refers to, "Cripples and Other Stories," presents a traumatized daughter. Her mother, "brilliant," her father, "fat on scotch, rich and clean," her doctor, a "comedian," each assembled to portray the history of a woman who remains "in her father's crib," afflicted with a wound she fears will show, shamed by her wasted life, and diminished by the disapproval of her family. This poem is not one of Sexton's best, but her question "In what ways am I a cripple still?" does perform differently from how yet another trauma story might. This poem can be read as an example of a different kind of cultural work that reports family trauma without having to be accountable to the limited criteria for representing the "truth" of abuse and the implications for being taught of "love too late."

At the start of this chapter, I indicated my intention to question the demands Winnicott placed on the "good-enough mother." As a woman who experienced the unnameable trauma of incest, Anne Sexton inherited a melancholic strain that was intensified by the demands that post–World War II America placed on middle-class women to be good-enough mothers, paradoxically leaving her vulnerable to feeling lost. The teaching life of Anne Sexton offers us a case of a pedagogy of reparation, in part because it is presents a teacher engaging in the study of problematic attachments. Her pedagogy is overlaid with emotions that underlie grief—sorrow and feelings of guilt, rage, and horror. Finally, Sexton also offers us a way to think differently about what is at stake in discussions about education that hold fast to regressive images of "good-enough mothers" who care for and nurture their students at the expense of their own subjectivities. The lectures in which she discusses her composing process are a generative site for reading the tensions involved in thinking about maternal metaphors in educational discourse and the lingering thematics of anxiety about maternal desire.

The metaphor of the "good-enough mother" is inadequate for educators because neither the mother nor the teacher can remain continually attuned, placid, contained, or unflappable. In addition, a student cannot become immersed in educative inquiry without experiencing conflict and a loss of equilibrium. Anne Sexton's use of personae building, as a rhetorical tactic, offers educators and students a process through which to shift from the Winnicottian metaphor of the "good-enough mother" to images of being and doing. At various moments during the composing process, the teacher may work like an actor rather than a container. As an actor, the teacher may provide stimulation—probing, elaborating, interpreting, or questioning the students' experiences and actively setting boundaries that structure the work of composing and responding to one another's work. By creating a place for students to struggle with the teacher's subjectivities as well as their own, writing can be used as a process of inquiry through which to achieve deeper level of interchange between them.

The implication that writing has for making reparation—for revising a life—is quite crucial to how I imagine Sexton's pedagogy. I am suggesting that Sexton's pedagogical narratives about her composing process combine to form a narrative of reparation that is used to recognize and work through ambivalent relationships with the lost object, in this case, "a safe and secure home." It is in this sense that the pedagogy of Anne Sexton constitutes a limit case in self-representation; for she presents her students with a series of inquiries into making reparation with a traumatized self through the "playful" act of writing and teaching. This work suggests that the notions of "good enough" set forth by Winnicott do not account for the difficult-to-engage subjectivities that are in fact necessary for reparative work. Thus, if we rely on the Winnicottian image of the "good-enough" maternal figure as teachers, we will unwittingly undermine the possibility for reparative work to take place in teaching and learning.

CHAPTER FIVE

Picturing the *Racial Innocence* of Anne Sexton's Pedagogy

... what the memory repudiates controls the human being. What one does not remember dictates who one loves or fails to love. What one does not remember ... contains the only hope, danger, trap, inexorability, of love—only love can help you recognize what you do not remember.

—*James Baldwin*

The lessons extended throughout the narratives documenting Sexton's teaching at Wayland High School during the 1967 to 1968 academic year continue to raise questions about academic taste: what it means to establish and sustain the proper distance between a student and teacher, and what pedagogical methods we use to engage in the evasion of history, and to sustain self-deception. Anne Sexton offers educators opportunities to move beyond the simple stance of examining how she made sense of teaching toward a consideration of how we use the practice of reading, writing, and teaching to make sense of ourselves. Sexton's teaching life tests our tolerance for certain kinds of understanding—she tests our capacity to hold certain difficult and uncertain ideas about ourselves as teachers and to think about what our professional identities are organized to exclude. To what are we emotionally resistant? What are we unable to acknowledge about our teaching lives? To address these questions, we will turn to a teaching journal that Sexton was required to keep for the Teachers and Writers Collaborative which she co-taught with Robert Clawson at Wayland High School in Wayland, Massachusetts, in 1967.[1]

My method for reading Sexton's journal is influenced most directly by the work of James Baldwin and Toni Morrison. In *Playing in the Dark: Whiteness and the Literary Imagination*, Morrison argues that the fabrication of a persona is a reflexive act that is an extraordinary meditation on the self, a powerful exploration of the fears and desires that reside in the writer's consciousness, a revelation of longing, terror, perplexity, shame, and magnanimity (1990, 51–52). Morrison insists on the importance of examining the conditions and processes that make it possible to compose personae in our scholarship and creative work. Throughout her writing, she suggests that we consider what it means to use someone else's life to make sense of our own. In using Sexton to understand my teaching life, I face fears of merging with a vulnerable teacher. To what extent do I employ Sexton on behalf of my own desire for a safe participation in love and loss? Entering my teaching life through the teaching life of Sexton poses difficult challenges. And so, as I return to Morrison, I find myself seeking out methods for reading her teaching life that will enable me to cast Sexton as a subject in her own right, an historical figure who calls forth our own reactions to her actions as Other, a figure whose pain, passion, and failures will reveal ourselves to ourselves without subsuming her integrity.

I begin this meditation by turning to what I have up until now neglected to address in Sexton's teaching life: her lack of racial consciousness. In my estimation, this is among the most vulnerable dimension of Anne Sexton's teaching life. Where Sexton, as a poet and teacher, is capable of articulating the disquieting and violent dimensions of post World War II domestic life—the anguish of addictions, myths of suburban security, incest, abortion, adultery, and her paradoxical desire to both hide and be known—she fails to admit discussions about race into her classroom.

The teaching journals kept by Anne Sexton during the time she taught at Wayland High School open up issues about racial innocence that are easy to ignore, given the apparent absence of race in the curriculum she designed with Bob Clawson and the Teachers and Writers Collaborative. Throughout his writings, James Baldwin calls on white persons to work toward understanding the deepest obstacles within ourselves, the most fragile, deplorable dimensions of our psyche. Borrowing from Baldwin (1955; 1985), it seems that Sexton's lack of racial awareness contributes to her remaining, on a symbolic level, "forever innocent," and consequently, ensconced in a vision of the world that is, in Baldwin's words, naïve. "Most people are not naturally reflective," notes Baldwin, "any more than they are naturally malicious, and the white man prefers to keep the black man at a certain human remove because it is easier for him thus to preserve his simplicity and avoid being called to account for crimes committed by his forefathers, or his neighbors" (1955, 166). Given these proclivities, Baldwin maintains that white persons "simply invite their own destruction, and anyone who insists on remaining in a state of innocence long after that innocence is dead turns himself into a monster" (174–175). In Baldwin's estimation, the monster lacks the necessary imagination and courage to address social injustices and inequities precisely because of a failure to experience the conversions necessary for identifying with the disowned, unwanted parts of themselves.

A STRIKING OMISSION

There are virtually no references to racial identity, racial tension, or black presence in Sexton's teaching documents—save for one exchange addressed later in the chapter. Such omissions are particularly remarkable given that Sexton began teaching at Wayland High School in 1967, just three years after President Johnson signed the Civil Rights Act of 1964. On February 21, 1965, Malcolm X was assassinated, one month before the March 7 march from Selma to the state capital of Montgomery, Alabama. This march, devised to protest the growing violence against civil rights activists throughout Alabama, resulted in the tragic murder of participants as they neared the Edmund Pettus Bridge. Footage of this attack was broadcast to the nation by ABC News, which interrupted the network's Sunday night movie, the premiere showing on television of *Judgment at Nuremburg* (a movie about bringing justice to the Nazis guilty of war crimes in World War II), to show fifteen minutes of raw and dramatic footage of the attack at the bridge (Isserman and Kazin, 1999, 136). No evidence indicates that Sexton watched the ABC broadcast, nor does she address the civil rights movement in any of the over one hundred personal correspondences she exchanged from 1963 to 1968.

In February 1965, Sexton suffered once again with acute depression. The letters she exchanged with Tillie Olsen, Anne Clarke, and James Dickey are full of news of her depression, medications, inquiries about jobs, the health of friends, and details about teaching. "The music . . . is playing strong," wrote Sexton to Anne Clarke on February 15, 1965.

> I was just laying on the ouch [couch] in my room looking out casually and I saw with shock the roof, snow lined, shining in the moonlight. When I saw that it hurt. I felt this awful pain. Does that make sense. A winter roof in the snow. [???] There it was, beautiful and terrible. I thought I'd tell you. It made me cry. I don't dare walk outside where the sky must hurt even extra with its full load of stars. The sky outside must ring . . . Rita [Ernst, her next-door neighbor from Newton] told me today that I've changed on thorazine. . . . She says I'm more childlike. She also says that she bets I haven't had one original idea since then. . . . Rita right. No ideas. None. Of my own. NOT ONE. . . . I'm not going to take anymore thorazine. I want to write poems! (1977, 258–259)

The sky indeed resounded with violence, civil disobedience, and death on the streets of Chicago, Brooklyn, Cleveland, and Dayton in 1965, yet Anne Sexton makes no mention of this unrest in her letters, nor does she direct her conscious attention to the violence erupting closer to home in Boston, New Haven, and Hartford, Connecticut. Perhaps Sexton was in far too much physical and emotional pain. She was suffering with epileptic-like seizures that included vomiting and passing out cold; the violence in her own home consumed her as did her daughters' growing desire and need to establish their independence from her. The physical and emotional condition of suffering Sexton expresses in her poetry and letters touches on the larger social condition at the time. As I write this, I think of Anne Sexton, confined to her house, lost in disorienting episodes of despair that at times seemed to bury her alive. In her New England home, walls enveloped her like damp sheets, drenched as they were in anxieties and inexplicable longings. The sensations Sexton recorded in her letters and poetry resonated with the fears of cold war America. Sexton feared being trapped in a house, as if the rooms would turn on her. These sensations are given form in many of the personae that circulate in her poetry, where the problems characters face are often figured in and through the problems of place, placement, and space. Writing about loss and failed love in her poem "Man and Wife," Sexton invokes the image of exile to capture the sense of routine dependence that draws her two protagonists together, over the years, in a house in the suburbs of Boston. "Now they are together, like strangers . . . eating and squatting together. . . . A soldier is forced to stay with a soldier because they share the same dirt and the same blows. They are exiles . . . soiled by the same sweat and the drunkard's dream" (1981, 116–117). In this prison home, white middle-class figures are impelled by a profound sense of fatal displacement.

Sexton's white, middle-class female body, medicated as it was with thorazine and librium, was apparently incapable of fully entering the body politic. More generally, we might say that, in the context of many of her poems and correspondences during this time, Sexton represents the somatic norm of the passive female citizen, possessing, as it were, a "servile soul" cultivated in fact to contain the fears and anxieties of the nation (Mills, 1997, 53–54).

It is against the social backdrop of the civil rights movement that Herbert Kohl and Anne Sexton began to plan which schools would participate in the Teachers and Writers Collaborative. The Teachers and Writers Collaborative took up its work within a systematic construction of a progressive project that was devoted to challenging a larger, national educational imperative designed to combat the perceived threats associated with the cold war.

Kohl was one of the key organizers of this project. By June 1967, he had received one year of funding from the U.S. Office of Education to construct pilot projects that would begin in September in select schools in New York City, Philadelphia, and, with Sexton and Clawson, Wayland, Massachusetts. This was an odd site to throw into the mix of urban, underfunded schools, but Sexton convinced Kohl that it was worthwhile to move into (and I paraphrase Sexton), white, WASP North America to see what would happen (Middlebrook, 1991, 274). "Why should such a good project be restricted to inner-city schools?" Sexton asked Kohl while they were attending a meeting of the board of directors of the Teachers and Writers Collaborative in New York. "None of the public schools have writers in residence. Why don't we go into white, WASP North America and see what happens there, too?" (274). Sexton is repeating herself when she says, "white WASP"—whiteness multiplied—whiteness times two. It is easy for a reader to ignore Sexton's neglect of the larger social, political movements of the time. In fact, it may be too easy to avoid her apparent lack of regard of black America all together.

※※※

In my struggle with the previous questions I posed, I continued to read Sexton's poetry and lecture notes over and over to locate racial tropes or signs of her attitudes toward race. I did find that during her teaching at Wayland High School, she and her students read Ralph Ellison's *Invisible Man*. But I also found that while she felt she could experience the book, she felt at a loss for discussing literature. Teaching literature made her feel uncomfortable, "off her stride" (Middlebrook, 1991, 286). There were no notes about her responses to this novel, only confessions of inadequacy. "I have now come to a passive position where I let the class happen," Sexton wrote in her journal, "The discussion of *Invisible Man* has put me off my stride because it is beyond me, and I am incapable of discussing it intelligently. I experience the book, but I can't discuss it." The words of Morrison come back to me: "What is the dark and abiding presence that is companion to the whiteness—a dark and abiding presence that moves the hearts and texts of American literature with fear and longing?" Why did *Invisible Man* disrupt Sexton's stride? The passivity that Sexton assumes in the face of this novel cannot be ignored, for in a subtle but powerful way, her position as passive in the midst of the African American presence this novel brings about reveals what Baldwin might describe as her own willful innocence, a desire, as Baldwin explains in *Notes of a Native Son*, "to nourish the illusion that there is some means of recovering the European innocence, of returning to a state in which black men do not exist" (1955, 174).

Sexton's passive treatment of Ellison's *Invisible Man* doubles over with meaning given that the nameless black narrator in this novel eloquently speaks of the ways in which whites must have a peculiar reciprocal "construction of [their inner eyes which renders black Americans invisible]" (96). The lack of visible presence and recognition given to black America in Sexton's and Clawson's curriculum is structured by what Charles W. Mills (1997) describes as the racial contract. It may seem odd—an unnecessary circuitous route—to turn to contract theory as I consider the lack of racial consciousness in Sexton's teaching journals, but this contract structures our teaching lives on the most intimate levels. To what do I consent to as a white teacher teaching in a predominantly white school? How culpable am I in accepting the privileges of whiteness? And how invisible is white domination and the assumptions that I make about what it means to be educated, sane, and healthy? The contract theory that is central to Western political theory is not a contract between everybody; rather, it is a contract established among, according to Mills, white people who in fact elect to attend to select realities at the expense of others as well as to obfuscate the "ugly realities of group power and domination" (3). The lack of active recognition that Sexton shows for Ellison's novel is, in my estimation, symptomatic of a specific kind of epistemological contract that is often tacitly assumed and referred to by Mills as an epistemology of ignorance. In his astute elaboration of the norms and procedures that constitute moral and factual knowledge within the framework of the racial contract, Mills argues that what is officially sanctioned as "real" diverges from the actual reality experienced by black Americans. "So here," notes Mills, "one has an agreement to misinterpret the world. One has to learn to see the world wrongly, but with the assurance that this set of mistaken perceptions will be validated by white epistemic authority, whether religious or secular" (18). In other words, given the terms of the racial contract, both evasion and self-deception become the epistemic norm.

The fact that Sexton refused to teach *Invisible Man* with the same investment as other literary works is particularly significant given the lack of visible presence allocated to black America in this curriculum. The racial contract, according to Mills, includes an epistemological contract, an epistemology of ignorance. "Recognition is a form of agreement," and by the terms of the racial contract, whites have agreed not to recognize blacks as equal persons. Thus, the white pedestrian who bumps into the black narrator at the start of this novel is a representative figure, "somebody lost in a dream world." "But didn't he control that dream world—which alas is only too real. And didn't he rule me out of it? And if he had yelled for a policeman, wouldn't I have been taken for the offending one? Yes, yes, yes!" (Ellison, 1975, 13–14). Similarly, Baldwin argues that white supremacy "forced white Americans into rationalizations so fantastic that they approached the pathological, generating a tortured ignorance so structured that one cannot raise certain issues with whites" (Baldwin, 1963, 172).

In 1967, Sexton failed to engage this text, thereby failing as a white academic, evading difficult issues, like others who find themselves thrown off their stride when confronted with material that is so deeply disturbing that it causes educators to stand before their students speechless. They then nervously stumble into discussions and rationalizations that rule out the possibility for addressing what they do not remember or what they insist on remaining ignorant of. In his book, *The Evidence of Things Not Seen*, James Baldwin addresses the impact that the forgotten histories of violence against black America has on all members of society. The issue, then, ironically lies in that which is not seen, and possibly not remembered. In Baldwin's words:

> What one does not remember dictates who one loves or fails to love. What one does not remember dictates, actually, whether one plays poker, pool, or chess. What one does not remember contains the key to one's tantrums or one's poise. What one does not remember is the serpent in the garden of one's dreams. What one does not remember is the key to one's performance in the toilet or the bed. What one does not remember contains the only hope, danger, trap, inexorability, of love—only love can help you recognize what you do not remember. (1985, xii–xiii)

Baldwin's point is that the histories we fail to remember or insist on remaining ignorant of insidiously feed our need to justify and perpetuate domination, control, and inequities. Moreover, this failure sabotages the possibility that we may ever experience love because, as Baldwin offers, it is only the Other who can be loved; the person who stands apart from us, but who creates a kind of productive irritation and doubt, provokes us to consider and explore the violence and horror of which we are all capable. But, in order to approach the Other, to begin to recognize her, we must be capable of understanding the most profound obstacles we face within ourselves (Benjamin, 1998a, 84). Baldwin's understanding of love resonates in strikingly familiar ways with the position taken up by D. W. Winnicott: "Only the concrete outside other can break up the closed energy system, only the other who can be moved but not coerced by us can take on some of what is too much for the self to bear. There is no question that we need the other—the question is only, can we recognize her?" (1969, 32).

The question of recognition plays out in teaching all the time. The teacher who fails to recognize that his students may not want for themselves what he wants for them not only remains undifferentiated, but unwittingly practices a pedagogy of self-deception, as so vividly portrayed by the relationship between Sexton and her poetry teacher, John Holmes. In such cases, students face pressure to become what they think the teacher wants them to become, to assimilate to her unwanted influence.

Also central to understanding the racial innocence structuring the teaching narratives of Anne Sexton during this time is the passive position she assumes so as to evade addressing race, despite her students' desire to pursue such issues. Ruth Frankenberg (1993) defines this passive attitude as one in which a person selects only those issues pertaining to difference that are good and comfortable for them to engage in. What is difficult, confusing, or throws one off kilter is ignored. Underlying this servile disposition, however, is an iron will—a strong refusal to recognize subjects of inherited privilege and the violence that this privilege brings about. But the refusal to recognize inherited privilege and violence requires enormous psychic work, for such recognition feels unbearable.

PRICILLA'S PAPER

Surprisingly enough, a few of Sexton's students attempted to raise issues of race and racism with her. Writing in her journal in November, Sexton dismisses one of her students, Pricilla Batten, as a young woman who holds onto a story of herself as "the dumbest." A close reading, however, reveals a different sort of story, for the details in Sexton's journal entries portray a series of images of a young woman trying to experiment with the performative "as if" position that Sexton used so often in her writing classes. In the following passage, Pricilla submits a draft of writing to Sexton in which she tries to approach and engage the black presence portrayed in *Invisible Man*. Sexton describes her reactions to Pricilla's writing:

Pricilla Batten comes in flapping her arms like a winged Biddlebaum saying "I can't write. You see I can't write. I can't." And hands in a non-assigned paper and when we read it, it's terrible. It's a prototype of the non-specific. It's about the Negro and the white and she writes as if she were a Negro. And she writes from no emotion and no knowledge. She writes a stereo-type, and today when I handed back the paper, she came at me again and said "You see, you see, I can't write, I can't write." I feel that I have done her a disservice and I lie to her and say, "Pricilla, you can write. But you haven't learned how to be specific yet. Once you learn that, you've got the whole rap beaten." And Pricilla looks at me and she's worried. And when she handed in her paper to me today, she said, "I tried. I really tried, but I can't write." And I know that I'd had a little failure. (Teachers and Writers Collaborative Archive, 16)

There are no details included in this entry about what transpired between Sexton and Pricilla during their initial discussion about this "non-assigned paper." How, for example, did Sexton address Pricilla's use of the "nonspecific"—or did she? Did Sexton explore with her students how to contour a stereotype—how to flesh it out and bring it to life? What is clear is that Sexton lied to Pricilla—giving her false praise and a little bit of advice to be" more specific," an ironic demand given Sexton's lack of specificity during this writing conference. What kind of specificity is Sexton after here? Does she come close to asking Pricilla to engage the black presence in this paper?

First, Pricilla's desire to take on a black persona raises concerns in Sexton, no doubt. Who is this black persona in question? What expressions, inflections, and pronouncements of black people did Pricilla attempt to portray? Why was this student struggling so to perform blackness? Ralph Ellison's *Invisible Man* opens with a sermon on the fluidity of blackness:

"Brothers and sisters, my text this morning is the 'Black of Blackness.'" In response, a congregation of voices respond: "That blackness is most black, brother, most black . . ."

"In the beginning . . ."

"At the very start," they cried.

"There was blackness . . ."

"Preach it . . ."

". . . and the sun . . ."

"The sun, Lawd . . ."

"was bloody red . . ."

"Red . . ."

"Now black is . . ." the preacher, shouted

"Bloody ..."

"I said black is ..."

"Preach it brother ..."

"... an' black ain't ..." (Ellison, 9–10)

The codes of blackness vary from context to context—that despite three centuries and two score years of colonialism, blackness remains a performance. But to describe Ellison's portrayal of blackness in the context of performance theory feels facile—like I'm moving too fast, striving to gain mastery of Sexton's response to Ellison and to Pricilla far too quickly. So, I slow down and reread this passage again and, as I do, I begin to wonder why Sexton feared addressing the classic question raised by Ellison's narrator: "What on earth was hiding behind the face of things?" What was hiding behind the face of Pricilla? Why did a teacher/poet who wrote of the vulnerability of the body, addictions, the pull to suicide, and the social dangers harbored in suburban America refuse to engage the social and spiritual dangers depicted by Ellison? Why did she refuse to explicate such a vital body of literature? Sexton's fear of exploring this issue with Pricilla and refusal to see how her "little failure" was in fact a profound failure of perception registered, as it were, in Pricilla's failed persona "about the Negro and the white" writing "as if she were a Negro." Sexton's refusal to engage the self-inflicted blindness that Ellison portrays in his novel, the complexities of racial collision and sexual violence, illuminates an aggressive strain in her pedagogy that Freud describes as a "narcissism of minor differences" (1930). Deborah Britzman astutely notes that this category, discussed by Freud (1998), is used to consider how aggression becomes the grounds for forging community and how the conditions for identification, abjection, and disassociation can, in her words, "divide and trouble the self" (30). In a perhaps "small and minor way," Sexton consoles herself with an image of Pricilla that enables her, as a teacher, to indulge herself for a moment in an excessive sense of self-regard. This indulgence is precisely what blinds Sexton to what she excludes from this curriculum. Despite Sexton's recognition that she has somehow failed Pricilla, Sexton casts Pricilla and her attempts to engage issues of race as a grotesque figure with anxious, nervous hands that beat, if we follow the reference of Sherwood Anderson's character of the schoolmaster, Wing Biddlebaum, like the wings of an imprisoned bird (Anderson, 30). Anderson's story of Wing Biddlebaum is really a story about hands. Wing Biddlebaum was a beloved teacher who touched his students with inspiring conversations and used his hands—caressing and touching his students' hair and stroking their shoulders—to "carry a dream into their young minds" (31). But tragedy strikes. Wing Biddlebaum is accused and beaten by the fathers of the town for putting his expressive, restless, and loving hands on their sons—beatings that were fueled by "shadowy doubts that had been in the men's minds ... and were galvanized into beliefs" (32). And so, in this odd scene, Sexton's student, Pricilla tries to write about race and, in return, Sexton casts her as a "winged Biddlebaum," referencing a character in a story in which charges of sexual molestation, homophobia, and societal fantasies run amok. Who does Sexton see in the face of Pricilla? Is Pricilla incapable of engaging racial tension, of being specific, or is Sexton? This apparently insignificant moment in the teaching life of Anne Sexton illuminates how the subtle but powerful strains of narcissism operate to interfere with a respectful recognition of the other and to project what we find intolerable about ourselves "into the other's identity" (Britzman, 1998, 29). Pricilla emerges as the "hidden face of Sexton's identity"—offering us a way to think about what the student who emerges as Other to us subjectively represents and how the Other can wear many faces. Just as Anderson's Wing Biddlebaum was tied up to the point of paralysis from using his hands—his most expressive "pennants of promise"—so Sexton finds herself at a loss, for her racial innocence leaves her submerged in a ghostly sea of doubts about her intellectual capacities and her knowledge about history.

"WRITE ABOUT WHAT YOU DON'T KNOW ABOUT WHAT YOU KNOW . . ."

One of the justifications Sexton offered for excluding writing assignments that engaged students in a discussion of racial consciousness pivots on the pedagogical assumption that students write best and with more rhetorical authority if they write about what they know. In other words, Sexton believed that students must write about what is familiar to them rather than attending to that which we designate as "not-part-of-self"—that which we cannot or refuse to see or what we are innocent of. "Yesterday," as Sexton recalls during the fall in her 1967 teaching journal, "we were discussing what kind of assignment they might like, and one of them brought up the colored people, one of them brought up burning draft cards, one of them brought up someone they knew very well that they could talk about. I prefer things they know about than things they don't know about. I don't want papers full of propaganda . . . I want papers full of concrete facts" (Teachers and Writers Collaborative Archive).

Given Sexton's logic, "colored people" and "draft cards" are not proper subjects to address because she assumes her white suburban students lack direct experience with them. Yet, what Sexton fails to note is that her students had recently read Grace Paley's poem "Six Boys Who Were Drafted from Brooklyn" and Ralph Ellison's *Invisible Man*. These texts no doubt stirred them, which created the opportunity for a political turn in the curriculum. Sexton's fear and phobic responses to the larger social world begin to fuse and mix and this fusion, like a dare, defies her capacity to transcend her unacknowledged, cast-out racial innocence.

In fact, Sexton relies on a misinterpretation of Grace Paley's advice to writers. Paley does not urge students to write about what they know; she advises them to write about what they *do not know* about what they know—a very different proposition from that offered by Sexton to her students at Way-land High School. Paley's position has the potential to create a space in the classroom for students to move in closer to the limits of their knowledge and understanding as well as approach the ignorance that frames the central body of what they claim to know about their lives, communities, families, and collective histories. The debates about personal writing in the academy often erupt into divisive arguments precisely because of this misunderstanding. Over the years, composition theorists who work within what has been designated as the "expressivist tradition" have argued not only that students should choose what they write about, but they should engage what they are interested in. Critics of personal writing often neglect this subtle point: Students should be encouraged to explore, invent, draft, revise, read aloud, and listen for what is half-spoken, for what is not fully present, but awaits articulation in the field of their interests, intimacies, and knowledge. In other words, they should write about what they *do not know* about what they know. This call resonates in the work of Janet Emig, Don Murray, and Peter Elbow; it is the through-line in a tradition of teaching writing that only barely recognizes its historical attachment to psychoanalysis and the power that the unconscious plays in teaching and writing.

Lad Tobin (2003) elaborates on the radical impact that psychoanalysis has had on the teaching of writing over the last thirty years. Tobin explores the academic anxieties and defenses that fuse arguments against writing personally, underscoring along the way that the unconscious plays a powerful role not only in the life of the writer, but in that of the teacher who reads student writing. Sexton's response to Pricilla Batten's paper presents a teacher who fails to adequately respond to her student's attempts to write about what she doesn't know about what she knows precisely because the teacher cannot bear losing mastery of the pedagogical situation. As stated earlier, Sexton is far too invested in her own excessive self-regard, her own desire to preserve what little intellectual confidence she had in this class. Sexton's psychic resistance to addressing issues of race reminds teachers not only of the racial opacity of the past—how astute some educators can be about failing to address histories they find disquieting—but also of the way that self-ignorance plays out in their teaching lives.

RACIAL INNOCENCE

The lessons offered to us in the journal Sexton kept while teaching at Wayland High School address, in the words of Baldwin, how we might "stroke the innocence out of ourselves." But these lessons take us, once again, on a circuitous route. Indeed, Sexton takes up the project of addressing what was made abject in post–World War II consciousness, and she does so at a great cost to her reputation and her family. Her poetry challenges the wholesale myths about American middle-class life at the time, capturing an underlying violence, chaos, and loneliness that took hold in too many suburban households. But, like many teachers, Sexton does not carry her project far enough, for she falls short of cultivating a sense of racial consciousness in her teaching. This failure causes her to evade what Mills calls on white intellectuals to recognize as "white domination, white power (what one writer in 1919 called the "whitetocracy" rule by whites), as a political system of exclusion and differential privilege, problematically conceptualized by the categories of either white liberalism or white Marxism" (131). These problematic concepts exert a strong influence on progressive pedagogies, conjuring up desires among white educators to protect and attend to the individual needs of white students. They conjure up desires among white progressive educators to evade, to literally refuse to substantially engage the buried histories of genocide and rebellions we find unspeakable. Whether we claim these evasions or not, whether we address what progressive education makes abject or not, these disavowals will shadow and outwit us. What liberates a person enough to face these disavowals, to claim evasions, to substantively engage the buried histories we are fearful of? Within these questions lie the key to unleashing the racial innocence that we cling to—an innocence that is not just about rhetoric. Our racial innocence pertains more, I believe, to a nuanced emotional consideration of fear of separation, abuses of power, passivity and antipathy for the Other.

The questions I pose resonate with a question posed by Roland Barthes (1977); it is a question I would like to pick up and elaborate on: "How can well-intentioned, . . . citizens end up enacting the racism of a domineering class?" Or to bring this question to bear on progressive pedagogy more directly, how can a reasonable, well-intentioned teacher enact the racism of a domineering class? Barthes offers an analysis of Western consciousness that is organized around a set of principle poses that I believe are useful for addressing the question of racial innocence in the teaching life of Anne Sexton and in our own.

The poses Barthes identifies were used by the white middle classes of the 1950s to render, organize, sustain, and reproduce what was perceived as a meaningful life in culture and society and they continue, notes Chela Sandoval (2000), "to tempt, inhabit, and shape not only the most obedient and deserving citizen-subject, but also the most rebellious agent of social change" (118). Each of these poses or *figurations* (a term Barthes also uses) offer a critical lens for appraising the passivity that sustains the racial innocence marking white educators' teaching lives. The teaching documents of Anne Sexton, particularly those she kept while teaching at Wayland High School, offer middle-class white teachers a curricular body full of citations of the poses elaborated on by Barthes. These poses are most likely used by each of us as easy masquerades for our identities as educators. I outline five rhetorical figures here in order to leave you with a catalogue of the poses that we use to inhabit white consciousness, particularly white consciousness in a colononizing mode.

1. *Inoculation.* The inoculation provides cautious, modest injections of difference. For example, Anne Sexton reads *Invisible Man* with her students, we advocate for affirmative action, and we create multicultural curricula.

Small, tidy portions of difference enter our teaching lives, and teach us to be admirably tolerant of difference. But, notes Barthes, these inoculations conceal the reality of class hierarchy and, consequently, numb out the citizenry. Sexton's proclivity to approach illness, adultery, incest, and death in unsuspecting ways placed her at the edge of societal norms for being a good mother and a good teacher. Yet, despite her resistance to the ideological demands made on middle-class women at the time, she remained merely stimulated by the work of black poets and writers, incapable of systematically engaging students and the faculty at large in substantive projects that would challenge her and their racial innocence.

2.   *Privation of history.* The passivity Anne Sexton felt in the presence of Ellison's novel also speaks to something larger: a passivity in consciousness about history. This *"privation of history,"* as described by Barthes, works by turning people away from the production of contemporary and past histories, an ignorance that is registered in Sexton's letters by the very absence of engagement or mention of the civil rights movement. This privation works in tandem with the process of inoculation, for, notes Sandoval, it "blithely turns its practitioners away from the very production of contemporary and past histories," in turn creating a sense of alienation in each of us as citizen–subjects that keeps us from recognizing that we do have the capacity to intervene in the world and to alter injustice.

3.   *Identification.* Found in Sexton's teaching documents and in much of our own work as educators, the process of identification that Barthes elaborates on occurs when the educator is comforted by either dismissing differences as insignificant or assimilating so that actual differences in others are recognized only as the self but, as Sandoval astutely reminds us, the self in other guises. The case of Pricilla Bratton offers us one case in which Sexton sees refracted in her student a strange version of herself—a teacher who fails to be specific about history. When the Other appears before us in horrifying ways that cannot be easily ignored, the good citizen–subject will do one of four things: (1) blind themselves, (2) ignore the differences, (3) deny the Other, or (4) transform the Other into themselves (Sandoval, 2000). This action is not only portrayed by Sexton, but by her teacher, John Holmes, when he reduced Sexton to an image of himself when criticizing her work. While Sexton indeed took on the image of the scandalous female poet who threatened normative notions of what it meant to be a good mother, teacher, and daughter, she also found, when confronted with the "scandalous threat" that race presented in the work of Ellison, that she could do nothing more than ignore difference or deny the presence of the other that may threaten what Barthes describes as the "security of the home." By ignoring history, one ignores any imperative that might introduce a reality that would challenge this notion of safety and, by refusing to

address difference, one is safely inoculated from the horrors of facing the
fears of absolute difference.

4. *Tautology.* The fourth pose elaborated on by Barthes is that of tautology—a
    device that defines like by like. Sexton uses tautological reasoning to make
    sense of her responses to Ellison by stating, "I felt myself thrown off my
    stride,"to which she may have also added, "that's just the way it is—that's
    all." She takes refuge in this state of confusion by using it to create a kind
    of impasse; there is no exploration of her statement, no pursuit of why she
    responds as she does—she leaves that to us. In her gloss of Barthes's text,
    Sandoval discusses this pose as one that certainly comes in handy if one is
    speechless, feeling powerless, or at a loss. If you are in need of a quick answer
    or explanation, then, as Sandoval instructs us, "take refuge in tautology, it of-
    fers the same feeing of refuge we take in fear, anger, or sadness" (121). Under-
    lying much of Charles Mills's discussion of the epistemology of ignorance
    is a tautological reasoning that enables citizens to believe that all Western
    knowledge is understood and justified by a logic that assumes that "history
    is history," "truth is truth," no questions asked, no proof is necessary.

    But there is more. Sexton offers us an example of the pose of neither-
    norisms in her admonition that she wants her students to write specifically
    with firm details because she does not want propaganda. Recall her nota-
    tion in her teaching journal:

    > We were discussing what kind of assignment they might like, and one
    > of them brought up the colored people, one of them brought up burning
    > draft cards, one of them brought up someone they knew very well and
    > that they could talk about. I prefer things they know about than things
    > they don't know about. I don't want papers full of propaganda . . . I want
    > papers full of concrete facts.

    In fact, this statement, while registering differences between what her
    students offered her as good ideas for writing assignments and what she
    wants from them, leaves Sexton free from having to choose between the
    contending power-laden realities of student and teacher. Here, Sexton re-
    duces the reality between what her students and she want to a formal
    opposite: propaganda versus concrete facts. She dismisses the historically
    produced differences between propaganda and what we deem as fact from
    discussion. These differences are registered, but finally ignored by Sexton.
    She becomes, in this strange instant, a "rational performer of 'neither-
    norisms.'" Her apparent neutrality to want factual papers creates an in-
    flexibility in this writing curriculum that works to support the dominant
    suburban order of things, excluding from discussion issues that lie beyond
    the edges of what her students know. For a moment, Sexton speaks with
    certainty, as if she were formally trained to present her reality as if there
    were no other.

5. *Quantification of quality.* And, finally, the fifth pose that Sexton takes up and resonates with Barthes's rhetoric of supremacy: *quantification of quality.* This pose positions educators as searching for more—more images, more emotion, more travel, commodities, cash, collections, knowledge, desire, homes, security—we can never have enough. The more flamboyant our effects, the deeper the meaning we have in our lives. This plays out in our search for increased quality of instruction, continual improvement plans, and life-long learning.

There is a strange turn here, however, in the pose that Sexton assumes as the teacher of weird abundance. She recognized the myth of plenitude, particularly as it pertained to post–World War II fantasies about the security of the family and paternal authority.[2] What she could not consciously recognize, however, were the effects that racism and colonization have on the perpetrators themselves. Feeling trapped in her home, but as if no place was home, Sexton suffered with acute episodes of agoraphobia. This affliction can be read on a figurative level as a failure to address history. The symptoms of anxiety that Sexton suffered with included spatial fear, leading to agoraphobia, claustrophobia, paralysis of movement, and temporal fear, leading to amnesia—the ultimate event—the failure to remember and historicize one's life. An important fact pertaining to the controversy over Anne Sexton's biography included serious debates over the audiotapes released by her psychiatrist Martin Orne to Diane Middlebrook, her biographer. Orne taped Sexton's psychotherapy sessions precisely because she could not remember them. Sexton would take the taped sessions home, listen to them, and transcribe them in large notebooks. The anxieties fused through these debates—which incidentally first drew my attention to her as a serious subject of study—are tied to Sexton's failure to remember and historicize her life. Sexton's seizing, alcoholic, and depressed body can be thus understood as the effects of living intimately with the demands posed by a particular economic, political, and cultural order, an order that coalesced into what Barthes considered the psychopathology of Western culture.

To challenge an order of things that keeps social alienation, violence, and inequity invisible is to challenge the hope and security of an integrated, whole, and firmly grounded self. Sexton was not meek about challenging the security of home and family. But the weird abundance that seeped out of the tightly wrought historical narratives, aphorisms, and tautological thinking taught in the colonizing mode deadened her sense of perception as a teacher, keeping vital aspects of the world around her invisible in her teaching life.

I imagine that there are lines in Ellison's book that touched Sexton, lines she understood deeply—although I have no way of knowing this. The lines that come back to me appear in the epilogue, when the invisible man recounts his lessons. He tells us that he now knows that he once lived a life in which he believed that "the world was solid and all the relationships herein. Now I know men are different and that all life is divided and that only in division is there true health." The invisible man warns his readers against conformity, and he speculates, on remembering an old gentleman looking for direction, that "to lose a sense of *where* you are implies the danger of losing a sense of *who* you are . . . very well, I've learned to live without direction" (568). To face profound difference—to engage the other that we find disquieting—is indeed to live a life divided, to challenge the myth of wholeness and safety. Anne Sexton cannot speak to us with wisdom about racial innocence, but she can instruct us in ways to attend to the racial innocence that is our own.

Epilogue

I ... believe that the personal is not the same as "private": the personal
is often merely the highly particular. I think the personal has fallen into
disrepute as sloppy because we have lost the courage and the vocabulary
to describe it in the face of the enormous social pressure to "keep it to
ourselves"—but this is where our most idealistic and our deadliest politics
are lodged, and are revealed.

—*Patricia Williams*

Anne Sexton believed in the curative properties of writing; she believed that
writing saved her life. Sexton felt that writing jarred her into a conscious
awareness of her complicity in living out and suffering through the plot of the
post–World War II American dream. Her history is imbued with unspeakable intrusions and pain—incest, suicidal despair, and instances of passively
enduring the exploitative "care" of psychiatrists. "One must make logic out of
suffering or one is mad," Sexton told her students at Colgate University. "All
writing of poems is sanity because one makes a reality, a sane world, out of
insane happenings."[1]

Teaching offered Sexton the opportunity to show others a route out of
depression and mental anguish. The route she took through poetry to ease her
despair was often criticized by figures such as A. R. Jones, who felt that Sexton
used writing to seek wholeness rather than awareness, thereby using poetry as
therapy rather than using the poetic form to compose art. In his estimation, this
need set her apart from her contemporaries: Sylvia Plath and Robert Lowell.
Responding to this criticism while teaching a course on poetry at Colgate University, Sexton notes:

> It is the split self, it seems to me, that is the mad woman. When writing you
> make a new reality and become whole. It is as if I were operating on myself
> and suturing on the arms and legs, placing the heart, settling the intestines.

> Much of my poetry is the poetry of a cripple, and yet the act of creation cures
> for a time. . . . In what ways am I a cripple still? [2]

Implicit in this statement is Sexton's sensitivity to the fact that a cure is always provisional and that the provisional qualities of cure are precisely what can generate a sense of awareness and a capacity to remain wide awake. The danger, as I discussed in earlier chapters, is that narratives of cure too often induce us to suppress grief, feelings of loss, sadness, and ambivalence about separation. Narratives of cure are attached to a consoling practice that has traditionally worked to normalize persons in pain. In earlier chapters, I have considered the ways in which Sexton challenges such narratives in her writing and in her teaching.

Louise DeSalvo (1999) traces the use of writing to cure—recognizing all along the potential dangers inherent in such a project. DeSalvo elaborates on a tradition of writing that Anne Sexton drew on as both a poet and a teacher, which was personal in nature. The urge to write, notes DeSalvo, is often provoked by pain, grief, or unnameable losses—subjective emotions felt by the poet. Elaborating on the work of Virginia Woolf, a writer who was her biographical subject for many years, DeSalvo discusses how Woolf's need to write came out of the pain and acute sense of shame that accompanied her childhood. Virginia Woolf wrote, notes DeSalvo, to "rub out" her father's violence and the shame she felt when she looked at her body. In "A Sketch of the Past," Woolf (1976) elaborates on why she turned to writing and what it accomplished for her: "I did for myself what psychoanalysts do for their patients. I expressed some very long and deeply felt emotion. And in expressing it I explained it and then laid it to rest" (DeSalvo, 1999, 76). DeSalvo explains that Woolf did not simply write to vent about her past or achieve a kind of cathartic discharge of emotion that would in turn usher her into normality. Writing that simply declares depression or describes the trauma of sickness, loss, or death can in fact function as a means through which to *evade* the narrative and emotional truths of our lives. Extending the work of James Pennebaker and Sandra Klihr Beall (1986), DeSalvo concludes that "to improve health, we must write detailed accounts, linking feelings with events. The more writing succeeds as narrative—by being detailed, organized, compelling, vivid, lucid—the more health and emotional benefits are derived from writing" (22). What criteria does DeSalvo suggest we use to determine if a narrative is sufficiently detailed, organized, compelling, or lucid? To what standards do we adhere? What in fact does DeSalvo mean by the term *narrative,* given that different discourses summon up their own distinctive tropes, figures, and meanings, thereby blocking out other imaginary communities and discursive practices?

On the surface, it appears that the "cure" offered by DeSalvo and practiced by figures such as Virginia Woolf and Anne Sexton resonates with the cure prescribed by Freud for the melancholic, a cure discussed in chapter 1. Freud (1919) submits that the anguish of the melancholic can be addressed through work that has cultural value. Once the melancholic can transfer her libidinal energy from the lost love object to work that is recognized in a social field, she can begin to successfully grieve her loss. This is in fact what Sexton's psychiatrist, Martin Orne, had in mind when he suggested that she take a poetry course at the Boston Adult Center for Education in 1957 after her first breakdown. And, indeed, poetry not only offered Sexton public recognition but a means to make a living.

A closer reading of DeSalvo's work suggests, however, a theory of writing that departs from Freud in important ways. DeSalvo is skeptical about writing that is used to achieve a "cathartic discharge of complex, pent-up feelings" (25). She believes that this approach to writing can in fact bring about a failure to hold difficult emotions and feel their impact. Throughout her work, DeSalvo makes an important distinction between writing simply to vent emotions and writing that enables the writer to hold emotions so that they can be examined and deeply felt (40). DeSalvo calls for reflection on the significance of the events one writes about, rerepresenting them so as to attain insight, even if this insight challenges dominant cultural norms or fails to translate into "legitimate" cultural work.

In my estimation, DeSalvo calls forth an important writing tradition that is associated with the work of Virginia Woolf and Walter Benjamin. What characterizes each of these writers' radical literary style—a style that I believe is evident in the work of Anne Sexton, specifically in the teaching journals and lecture notes she kept while teaching at Wayland High School and Colgate University—is an intentional reproduction of an ambivalent cognitive mode that combines mastery with vulnerability. Each of these writers articulate the interdependency between *failure*—what Sexton once referred to after her failed trip to Europe as the "ultimate American humiliation"—and *expertise*. Benjamin (1978) comments on this ambivalent cognitive state: "It is likely that no one ever masters anything in which he has not known impotence; and if you agree you will also see that this impotence comes not at the beginning of or before the struggle with the subject, but at the heart of it" (1978). Benjamin insists that personal writing that restores subjectivity to history, that is, linking our selves as it were to a larger collective, creates scenes of writing that make the human body a subject of history.

Throughout this book I have emphasized that life writing, which has curative properties but does not normalize the writer, discretely names the penetrating interdependencies of the historical subject and the subjects of history. The kind of writing DeSalvo describes and Sexton practices with her students implies that the subjectivity of the writer and teacher is restored through a process of articulation and recognition that elaborates on the body and its affective, social, historical, and political situation. Sexton's journal and lecture notes offer prime examples of just this kind of writing, for she attempts to address the shame, fear, and disgust that teaching inevitably stirs within us as teachers, and, in doing so, she articulates a method for pursuing those aspects of our emotional lives we ordinarily would turn away from. Writing during World War II, rhetorician Kenneth Burke called this rhetorical approach to writing "equip-ment for living" because it cultivated a temperament for revision—a process of "let us try again" keep revising, amplifying, expanding our self—a temperament that combines vulnerability with mastery and control (see Warnock, 1997, 37).

Sexton's work shows us the importance of using revision, not only as a textual art, but as a life skill. It is also the series of paradoxical lessons of writ-ing personally, but not about ourselves, that is Sexton's inimitable pedagogical legacy.

Notes

INTRODUCTION

1. For an extended discussion of the ways in which Sexton's poetic performances resonated with the contemporary performances of "hysteria," staged by figures such as Orlan, Cindy Sherman, and Sue Maddon, see Elisabeth Bronfen (1998).

2. See "My Sweeney, Mr. Eliot": Anne Sexton and the Impersonal Theory of Poetry" by Joanna Gill, *Journal of Modern Literature*, 27.1, September 2003, 35–36. Accessed at: http://muse.jhu.edu/journals/journal_of_modern_literature/v027/27/1gill.html.

3. On the issue of the place of the personal in teaching and scholarship within the context of curriculum theory, see also Deborah Britzman (1998), Sharon Todd (2003), and Ursula Kelly (2004).

4. For a discussion about the politics of the personal as it is inscribed by academics within the postindustrial university, see Susan Talburt and Paula Salvio (2004).

5. For an extended discussion about the logic of control and anxiety about sexuality that structures early childhood discourses, see the work of Jonathan Silin (1995), Gaile S. Cannella (2000), and Valerie Walkerdine (2000).

6. For an insightful analysis of the traps of self-deception in teaching, see Jim Garrison (1997).

7. See *Between Women: Biographers, Novelists, Critics, Teachers and Artists Write About Their Work with Women*, edited by Carol Ascher, Louise DeSalvo, and Sara Ruddick (New York: Routledge, 1984).

8. See Freud, 1919. All quotations from this introduction will be taken from the corrected reprint of this edition in Sigmund Freud, *Art and Literature*, The Pelican Freud Library, vol. 14, edited by Albert Dickson (Harmondsworth: Penguin Books, 1985, 335–376).

9. Freud's writing on the uncanny has been scrutinized for its own uncanny lapses. See, for example, Helene Cixous, "Fiction and Its Phantoms: A Reading of Freud's Das Unheimliche," *New Literary History* 7 (Spring 1976): 525–548; Samuel Weber, "The Sideshow, or: Remarks on a Canny Moment," *Modern Language Notes* 88 (1973): 1102–1133; Sara Kofman, *The Childhood of Art: An Interpretation of Freud's Aesthetics*, translated by

Winifred Woodhull (New York: Columbia University Press, 1988), from *L'Enfance de l'art* (Paris: Payot, 1970).

CHAPTER ONE

1. This chapter portrays an example of what Leigh Gilmore refers to as the *autobiographical demand*, a form of critical life writing in which the demands of autobiography, the call to tell *my* story, and the demands of biography, the call to tell *your* story, coincide. Gilmore argues that the auto/biographical demand presents a narrative dilemma because it both divides and doubles the writer. At the moment that I begin to tell the story of Sexton's teaching life, aspects of my life surface and demand articulation. These demands provoke a sense of instability in my writing and pose emotional and rhetorical constraints that auto/biography manages by mingling a range of forms: biography, memoir, autobiography, poetry, the essay, and theoretical writing. Throughout this chapter, I draw on Gilmore's concept to explore the ways in which the auto/biographical demand places in relief the double bind faced by a writer who inherits the unavoidable tasks to speak for the dead and to properly address a traumatized past that is unspeakable because it remains shrouded in shame. The dead, Gilmore goes on to remind us, make demands on the living; they surface in our dreams, our current relationships, through writing, teaching, and scholarship. But to understand these demands, the writer must distinguish between her story and theirs and, in so doing, must navigate through the delicate tensions that are inherent in the narrative structure of auto/biography—the tension between telling stories and sustaining family loyalties, articulating family secrets and properly mourning a traumatized past (see Gilmore, 2001).

2. Leverich to Sexton. Found in Anne Sexton archives at the Harry Ransom Humanities Research Center (hereafter abbreviated HRHRC), University of Texas, Austin.

3. Ibid.

4. Ibid.

5. Lecture notes, Colgate University, HRHRC.

6. Leverich, HRHRC.

7. Abraham and Torok develop the concept of *cryptonymy* to reconfigure the Freudian notion of the unconscious as a psychic crypt, a kind of tomb or vault harboring the not fully confronted "phantoms" or secrets from the analysand's family history. For more on the concept of the *fantome* and cryptic incorporation, see Peggy Kamuf, "Abraham's Wake," *Diacritics* 9, no. I (1979): 32–43, and Nicholas Rand's translator's introduction to *The Wolf Man's Magic Word: A Cryptonymy* (Minneapoljis: University of Minnesota Press, 2005). Also, for further commentary on Abraham and Torok, see Esther Rashkin, *Family Secrets and the Psychoanalysis of Narrative* (Princeton: Princeton University Press, 1992). For a discussion about the implications melancholia has on student writing and the difficulties students face in locating an object of address when writing about loss, see Mary Hallet's "Personal Effects: Grief, Loss and the Pedagogies of Writing," *Journal of Curriculum Theorizing*, 15(1999).

8. Sexton held the Crawshaw Chair in Literature at Colgate University from May–June, 1972; from lecture notes at Colgate University, HRHRC.

9. Diane Wood Middlebrook is cautious about concluding that Ralph Harvey, Anne Sexton's father, made sexual advances toward her. However, Sexton's memories of this abuse do surface in her psychiatric tapes and in her work. Middlebrook writes, "Was Sexton's report a memory or a fantasy? This question achieved great importance in her therapy, and in her art, but it cannot be answered with certainty. The evidence for its actuality lies chiefly in the vividness and frequency of her descriptions during trance states. Moreover, Sexton's symptoms and her behavior—in particular, the dissociative states that were so prominent a feature in her case, her tendency to sexualize significant relationships, and the fluidity of the boundaries she experienced between herself and other people—fit the clinical picture of a woman who has undergone sexual trauma. From a clinical point of view, her doubts about this memory were not evidence that it did not happen" (1991, 57). Middlebrook goes on to note that Sexton's accounts did vary and that her memories of abuse surfaced in therapy when she was reading and writing about incest, especially during active work on a play that had, as its central conflict, an incestuous episode. "As Sexton frequently commented," notes Middlebrook, "once she had put a memory into words, the words were what she remembered. Thus she could give dramatic reality to a feeling by letting it generate a scene and putting that scene into words for Dr. Orne while in a trance" (57). Dawn Skorczewski, however, notes the danger inherent in questioning the evidence of such abuse, arguing that to suggest that Sexton merely dramatized her memories of incest through her art is to sanction sexual violence. For a substantive and moving discussion about the educative value of teaching incest narratives, see *Authoring a Life* by Brenda Daly (Albany: State University of New York Press, 1998).

10. Lecture notes, Colgate University, HRHRC.

11. Madeleine R. Grumet discusses the epistemic and pedagogical implications of composing educational autobiography by conjugating theory with literature, history, and other people's stories in "Scholae Personae: Masks for Meaning" in *Pedagogy: The Question of Impersonation,* edited by Jane Gallop (Bloomington: Indiana University Press, 1995).

12. For an extensive discussion on the concept of a "return of a difference," see Elizabeth Ellsworth, *Teaching Positions: Difference, Pedagogy and the Power of Address* (New York: Teachers College Press, 1997).

13. To "work something through" is to repossess or reclaim emotions that we have become estranged from; this work makes present what was otherwise encrypted or buried in the past so that it can in fact be felt as emanating from one's own person, one's own body. Thus, "working through" memories entails the gradual knowing of the disaffected material that comes from our own being. In his essay, "Remembering, Repeating and Working Through," Freud describes this process as one that must "allow the patient time to become more conversant with this resistance with which he has now become acquainted, to work through it, to overcome it, by continuing, in defiance of it, the analytic work according to the fundamental rule of analysis" (*Standard Edition of the Complete Psychological Works of Sigmund Freud, vol. 12,* edited and translated James Strachey, London: Hogarth Press and Institute of Psychoanalysis, 1958, 155).

14. See Elaine Scarry (1985). Scarry not only explores the political implications inherent in the inexpressibility of physical pain, but also the role of the imagination in coming to terms with the limits of language, arguing that "the human being who creates

on behalf of the pain in her own body may remake herself to be one who creates on
behalf of the pain originating in another's body; so, too, the human beings who create
out of pain (whether their own or others') may remake themselves in a way that dis-
tributes the facts and responsibilities of sentience out into the external world" (324–325).
Scarry's theory of *making* offers important insights into the potential implications of
Sexton's poetry, suggesting that her imaginative work as a poet, teacher, and playwright
distributed unspeakable facts and responsibilities of sentience into an external world in
an effort not only to articulate loss, but to move away from pain, toward the boundaries
of self-transformation.

15. Lecture notes, Colgate University, HRHRC.

16. Personal communication with Bruce Berlind, Colgate University, 1996.

17. Lecture notes, Colgate University, HRHRC.

18. For an extended discussion of the double body, see Peggy Phelan (1993, 172;
1996, 63).

19. See Fanon, 1952.

20. In *Unmarked: The Politics of Performance*, Peggy Phelan elaborates a form of
remembering that does not seek to reproduce the lost object but rather rehearses and
repeats "the disappearance of the subject who longs always to be remembered" (1993,
147). The crucial point underlying Phelan's argument is that to simply describe what or
whom we have lost does not reproduce the object; instead these descriptions remind us
how loss acquires meaning and can indeed generate recovery, not of the lost object, per
se, but for the person who remembers. The economy of performance spurs memory on,
encouraging memory to become present, yet these memories cannot be contained or
controlled.

CHAPTER TWO

1. Throughout this chapter, I draw on the teaching documents of Anne Sexton,
all of which are housed in the Harry Ransom Humanities Research Center (hereafter
abbreviated HRHRC) at the University of Texas, Austin.

2. For an extensive discussion of the improvisational qualities inherent in de
Certeau's tactical maneuvers, see Mary Russo (1994). For a compelling application of
de Certeau's tactics and strategies to pedagogy in higher education, see Susan Talburt
(1999).

3. Lecture notes, Colgate University, HRHRC.

4. Ibid.

5. The way in which unspoken histories are nested in the details of domestic life is
explored in Homi Bhaba's (1994, 1–18) discussion of the uncanny.

6. See Oliver (1993, 72–77).

7. For further discussion of the process of reduplication with respect to identity,
loss, and mourning, see Julia Kristeva (1989).

8. Lecture notes, Colgate University, HRHRC.

9. Here I refer to the ways in which modernity has been haunted by a myth of
transparency of the self to nature, of the self to other, of all selves to society—a form

of transparency figured, for example, in the trope of the panopticon, its walls hiding no secrets, particularly among schoolchildren and prisoners. Another image that comes to mind is the ideology of the glasshouse of the soul, described by Anthony Vidler as a psychogeographic glasshouse that parallels the ideology of the glasshouse of the body—an aerobic glasshouse—that provoked artists such as Marcel Duchamp, Man Ray, and Georges Bataille to favor, as I do, a little dust, interfering with what Batille describes as a "sicken cleanliness and logic" refusing to save us from "nocturnal terrors." See Georges Bataille, "Architecture," in *Oeuvres completes* (Paris: Gallimard, 1970), 1: 171, first published in Documents 2 (May 1929): 117. See also Anthony Vidler (1992).

10. Peter M. Taubman (1990) analyzes the psychic dynamics, distances, and prox-imities that come into play when teachers work to negotiate the "proper distance" be-tween themselves and their students.

11. See Melissa F. Zeiger (1997) for a substantive analysis of the normative implica-tions of Freud's concept of mourning. Zeiger discusses the ways in which the genre of elegy, as a male initiation ritual that indeed stands for being a successful male subject, bars women and attempts to distance loss and femininity. Zeiger builds on the work of Louise Fradenburg, "Voice Memorial": Loss and Reparation in Chaucer's Poetry, *Exemplaria,* 2 (March 1990): 184.

12. See Richard Schechtner's (1985) discussion of performative consciousness. For a discussion of Freud's essay "On the uncanny" see Helene Cixous, "Les Fictions et ses fantomes," *Poetique* 3 (1972): 199–216.

13. For an extended discussion of the anxieties about the female body inherent in Bakhtin's romantic portrayals of the grotesque, see Mary Russo (1994).

CHAPTER THREE

1. The work of, for example, Dale Bauer (1988, xiv–xv), Mimi Orner (1993), and Sharon Todd (2003) addresses the subtle but most powerful ways in which liberatory pedagogy can work to undermine students' ontological state without their consent.

2. Middlebrook describes John Holmes as a devoted teacher, and discusses the impact that he had on the writing of the young poets he taught in her biography of Anne Sexton (1991, 500–512).

3. For an eloquent explication of Freud's concept of "narcissism of a minor differ-ence" and its application to educational communities, see Britzman (1998, 12).

4. For an extended discussion about the correlation the concept of the Other has to the ethical problem of respect for persons and the political problem of nonviolence, see Benjamin (1998b).

5. Again, see Britzman (1998) for an analysis of the ways in which educational communities are formed through aggressive practices of exclusion.

6. From materials in the Anne Sexton archives located at the Harry Ransom Humanities Research Center (hereafter abbreviated HRHRC), University of Texas, Austin.

7. On the one hand, I might argue that my methodological approach to writ-ing about Sexton is associated with what Sidonie Smith (1987), in her early work on women's autobiography, describes as speaking outside of the prevailing framework of

individuality. From this point of view, women writing auto/biographically represent themselves in ways that emphasize interpersonal, present connections to the world and to other significant figures in their lives. This approach to representation stands apart from the economy of self-hood that male writers draw on—one that more generally emphasizes the Anglo democratic ideal of individuality. My prosaic portraits of Sexton can be read as portraits that illuminate my teaching life as well as hers—of articulating at least two histories at once.

On the other hand, however, I find that in writing about Sexton, I compose a narrative of concealment. In other words, I use writing as a way unconsciously to hide aspects of my history, leaving those areas of my past that are unbearable to lead a secret life. And in this act of concealment, I find myself eclipsing aspects of my past in much the same way that Holmes, in his pedagogical relationship with Sexton, eclipsed aspects of his. To admit that the relationship between Anne Sexton and John Holmes bears certain resonances to me, that I find the patterns in their relationship uncanny, is to admit to narcissistic attachments that I have harbored all along—fears of losing control, of losing mastery, and anxieties about the limits of my intellectual capacities. Moreover, my admission provokes me seriously to consider why I became interested in this teacher and his apparently unruly student. Among the questions I explored during this project are: What remains half-spoken in my writing and my teaching life that I associate with the pedagogical relationship between Anne Sexton and John Holmes? And why would this be important to attend to? See *Between Women*, edited by C. Ascher, L. DeSalvo, and S. Ruddick (1984) for an analysis of the ways in which female scholars conceptualize their work on women and the "double-voiced" narratives that emerge, narratives that speak of the writer as much as they speak about the writer's subject. Also see the work of C. Steedman (1987, 17).

8. Sexton on Tillie Olsen: During the time that Sexton was a Bunting Fellow at Radcliffe, she became close friends with Tillie Olsen. When Sexton reflected on her two years at the Radcliffe Institute, she remembered Olsen's presentation of her work, which at the time pertained to *Silences*, as having had the most profound impact on her. In an interview with Martha White, a social psychologist who studied the Bunting Fellows at the time, she said, "Tillie's seminar probably changed my writing as much as anything. She put in a theory of failure, how you can waste yourself. At that moment I was so worried about failure. Artists always are. . . . Tillie rededicates you. That's what she did for me; I couldn't speak afterward, I was in a state of shock. Tillie's seminar went way overtime, but if anyone had stopped her, I would have chopped their head off" (from interview with Martha White, July 1963, "Tillie's Seminar").

9. The father I invoke here resonates with the "imaginary father," described by Julia Kristeva in *Tales of Love* and *Black Sun*. She elaborates on Freud's brief description of the "father in [one's] own prehistory," before the Oedipal process, with whom the child makes "a direct and immediate identification" (Freud, 1923, 639). This father differs from the Oedipal father the child will later encounter. "He" is a "father–mother conglomerate" (Kristeva, 1983, 40), who offers the child "a warm but dazzling, domesticated paternity," while the Oedipal father is a "stern" one associated with separation and judgment (46). Both fathers, the imaginary and the symbolic, are actually separate aspects of a single process that is necessary for the child to identify with if she is to learn to connect abstract symbols with emotions (1989, 23–24). According to Kristeva, both the imaginary father of love and the symbolic father associated with the symbolic order are necessary if the child is to learn to endow words with genuine meaning.

10. For a discussion of rivaling as a rhetorical practice through which to deliberate over social inequities, see Flower (2000).

11. A letter to Schopenhauer to Goethe, November 1815.

CHAPTER FOUR

1. Wendy Atwell-Vasey, personal communication, summer, 2005. Also, for an extended discussion about the place of literary studies in the work of trauma, see Brenda Daly, 1998.

2. The letter written by Sexton's nieces can be located in "The Sexton Tapes" by Samuel Hughes, Pennsylvania Gazette, 1991. Assessed at: www.dianemiddlebrook.com/sexton/tpg12-91.html.

3. Interview with Samuel M. Hughes, Pennsylvania Gazette, 12–91.

4. Kavaler-Adler draws on object relations theory to more fully appraise the quality of treatment that Sexton received from her psychiatrists, and to raise questions about the potential the creative process, as used by Sexton, had for reparative work. Also, see Berman (1999) for an analysis of the literature of suicide.

5. Found in Anne Sexton archives at the Harry Ransom Humanities Research Center (hereafter abbreviated HRHRC), University of Texas, Austin.

6. Ibid.

7. Ibid.

8. Ibid.

9. Ibid.

10. Ibid.

CHAPTER FIVE

1. Although I do not elaborate on the relationship between the ideology of nurturance and racial innocence in this book, I suspect that the passivity associated with the history and practice of nurturance contributes in subtle ways to cultivating the racial innocence that Baldwin so eloquently discloses in his work. This is an area in need of serious study.

2. For an analysis of the "failure of paternal authority," see Bronfen (1998).

EPILOGUE

1. Crawshaw lectures notes, from the Anne Sexton archive at the HRHRC.

2. Lecture notes, Colgate University, HRHRC.

Bibliography

Abraham, Nicholas, and Maria Torok. 1994. *The Shell and the Kernal* (vol. I), edited and translated by Nicholas T. Rand. Chicago: University of Chicago Press.

Allison, Dorothy. 1992. *Bastard Out of Carolina*. New York: Dutton.

Anderson, Sherwood. 1919 [1976]. "Hands" in *Winesburg, Ohio*. New York: Penguin.

Ascher, Carol, DeSalvo, Louise and Ruddick, Sara (editors). 1993. *Between Women: Biographers, Novelists, Critics, Teachers and Artists Write About Their Work on Women*. London: Routledge.

Atwell-Vasey, Wendy. 1998. *Nourishing Words: Bridging Private Reading and Public Teaching*. Albany: State University of New York Press.

Babcock, Barbara (ed.). 1978. *The Reversible World: Symbolic Inversion in Art and Society*. Ithaca, NY: Cornell University Press.

Bakhtin, M. M. 1981. *The Dialogic Imagination*. Edited by Michael Holquist, translated by C. Emerson and M. Holquist. Austin: University of Texas Press.

———. 1965. *Rabelais and His World*. Translated by Helene Iswolsky. Bloomington: Indiana University Press.

Baldwin, James. 1985. *The Evidence of Things Not Seen*. New York: Holt, Rinehart and Winston.

———. 1963. Ref Ch 5

———. 1955. *Notes of a Native Son*. Boston: Beacon Press.

Barthes, Roland. 1977. "Writers, Intellectuals, Teachers." In *Image-Music-Text*, translated by Stephen Heath, 190–215. New York: Hill.

Bauer, Dale M. 1988. *Feminist Dialogics: A Theory of Failed Community*. Albany: State University of New York Press.

Bellamy, Elizabeth. 1997. *Affective Genealogies: Psychoanalysis, Postmodernism, and the "Jewish Question" after Auschwitz*. Lincoln and London: University of Nebraska Press.

———. 1988. *The Bonds of Love: Psychoanalysis, Feminism, and the Problem of Domination*. New York: Random House.

———. 1998. *Shadow of the Other: Intersubjectivity and Gender in Psychoanalysis*. New York: Routledge.

Benjamin, Walter. 1978. *Reflections*. Edited by Peter Demetz translated by Edmund Jephcott. New York: Harcourt Brace.

Berman, Jeffrey. 1999. In *Surviving Literary Suicide*. Amherst: University of Massachusetts Press.

Berube, Michael, and Cary Nelson (eds). 1995. *Higher Education Under Fire: Politics, Economics, and the Crisis of the Humanities*. New York: Routledge.

Bhaba, Homi. 1994. *The Location of Culture*. New York: Routledge.

Bleich, David. 1998. *Know and Tell: A Writing Pedagogy of Disclosure, Genre, and Membership*. Portsmouth, NH: Heinemann.

Boldt, Gail M., and Salvio, Paula M. 2006. *Love's Return: Psychoanalytic Essays on Childhood, Teaching and Learning*. New York: Routledge.

Bollas, Christopher. 1995. *Cracking Up: The Work of Unconscious Experience*. New York: Hill and Wang.

———. 1994. *Being a Character: Psychoanalysis and Self Experience*. New York: Hill and Wang.

Bourdieu, Pierre. 1984. *Distinction: A Social Critique of the Judgment of Taste*. Translated by Richard Nice. Cambridge: Harvard University Press.

Boyers, Robert. 1978. "Live or Die: The Achievement of Anne Sexton." In *Anne Sexton: The Artist and Her Critics*, edited by J. D. McClatchy, 204–215. Bloomington and London: Indiana University Press.

———. 1974. *Contemporary Poetry in America: Essays and Interviews*. New York: Schocken Books.

Bratton, Pricilla. Anne Sexton Teaching Journal, Teachers and Writers Collaborative Archive, New York City.

Brecht, Bertolt. 1964. *Brecht on Theatre*. Translated by John Willet. London: Methuen.

Britzman, Deborah P. 2006. "Sigmund Freud, Melanie Klein and Little Oedipus: On the Pleasures and Disappointments of the Enlightenment." In *Love's Return: Psychoanalytic Essays on Childhood, Teaching and Learning*, edited by Gail Boldt and Paula M. Salvio, pg nos. New York: Routledge.

———. 1998. *Lost Subjects, Contested Objects: Toward a Psychoanalytic Inquiry of Learning*. Albany: State University of New York Press.

Britzman, Deborah, and Alice Pitt. 2004. "Pedagogy and Clinical Knowledge: Some Psychoanalytic Observations on Losing and Refinding Significance." *Journal of Advanced Composition* 24 (2): 353–374.

Brodkey, Linda. 1996. *Writing in Designated Areas Only*. Minneapolis: University of Minnesota Press.

Bronfen, Elisabeth. 1998. *The Knotted Subject: Hysteria and Its Discontents*. Princeton: Princeton University Press.

Butler, Judith. 1997. *The Psychic Life of Power: Theories of Subjection*. Stanford: Stanford University Press.

———. 1993. *Bodies That Matter*. New York: Routledge.

———. 1990. *Gender Trouble: Feminism and the Subversion of Identity*, New York: Routledge.

Chodorow, Nancy. 1995. "Gender as Personal and Cultural Construction." *Signs* 20(Spring): 516–544.

Cannella, Gaile S. 2000. "The Scientific Discourses of Education: Predetermining the Lives of Others—Foucault, Education and Children." *Critical Issues in Early Childhood* 1(1): 36–44.

Colburn, Steven E. 1988. *Anne Sexton: Telling The Tale*. Ann Arbor: University of Michigan Press.

Crapanzo, Vincent. 1990. "On Dialogue." In *The Interpretation of Dialogue*, edited by Tullio Maranhao, 269–291. Chicago: University of Chicago Press.

Daly, Brenda. 1998. *Authoring Life: Women's Survival In and Through Literary Studies*. Albany: State University of New York Press.

de Certeau, Michel. 2002. *The Practice of Everyday Life*. Berkeley: University of California Press.

———. 1984. *The Practice of Everyday Life*. Berkeley: University of California Press.

Deleuze, Gilles. 1988. *Foucault*. Edited and translated by Sean Hand. Minneapolis: University of Minnesota Press.

Deleuze, Gilles, and Felix Guattari. 1980. *A Thousand Plateaus: Capitalism and Schizophrenia*. Translated by Brian Massumi. Minneapolis: University of Minnesota Press.

De Laurentis, Teresa. 1987. *Technologies of Gender: Essays on Theory, Film, and Fiction (Theories of Representation and Difference)*. Bloomington: Indiana University Press.

DeSalvo, Louise. 1999. *Writing as a Way of Healing: How Telling Our Stories Transforms Our Lives*. Boston: Beacon Press.

Dworkin, Andrea. 1974. *Woman Hating*. New York: Penguin.

Edgerton, Susan. 2002. "Learning to Listen and Listening to Learn: The Significance of Listening to Histories of Trauma." Paper presented at the Philosophy of Education Society. Vancouver, Canada

Edgerton, Susan, et al. 2004. *Imagining Higher Education: The Academy in Popular Culture*. New York: Routledge.

Eigen, Michael. 1977. "On Breathing and Identity." *Journal of Humanisitc Psychology* 17: 35–39.

———. 1993. *The Electrified Tightrope*. Northvale. NJ: Jason Aronson.

Ellison, Ralph. 1947. *Invisible Man*. New York: Modern Library.

Ellsworth, Elizabeth. 1997. *Teaching Positions: Difference, Pedagogy and the Power of Address*. New York: Teachers College Press.

Emigh, John. 1996. *Masked Performances: The Play of Self and Other in Ritual and Theatre*. Philadelphia: University of Pennsylvania Press.

Epstein, Mark. 1995. *Thoughts Without a Thinker: Psychoanalysis from a Buddhist Perspective*. New York: Basic Books.

Fanon, Franz. 1952. *Black Skin, White Masks*. New York: Grove Press.

Fein, Richard. 1967. "The Demon of Anne Sexton." The English Record 18 (October): 16–21.

Felman, Shoshanna. 1993. *What Does a Woman Want?: Reading and Sexual Difference*. Baltimore and London: The Johns Hopkins University Press.

Felman, Shoshanna, and Dori Laub. 1992. *Testimony: Crises of Witnessing in Literature, Psychoanalysis, and History*. New York: Routledge.

Flower, Linda, Elenore Long, and Lorraine Higgins. 2000. *Learning to Rival: A Literate Practice for Intercultural Inquiry*. Mahwah, N.J: Erlbaum.

Foucault, Michel. 1980. *The History of Sexuality. Vol. 1: Introduction*. Translated by Robert Hurley. New York: Vintage.

Frankenberg, Ruth. 1993. *White Women, Race Matters: The Social Construction of Whiteness*. Minneapolis: University of Minnesota Press.

———. 1975. *Discipline and Punish: The Birth of the Prison*. New York: Vintage.

Frank, Arthur. 1995. "Lecturing and Transference: The Undercover Work of Pedagogy." In *Pedagogy: The Question of Impersonation*, edited by Jane Gallop, 28–35. Bloomington: University of Indiana Press.

Freud, Sigmund. 1989. "Mourning and Melancholia." In *The Freud Reader*, edited by Peter Gay, 628–658. New York: W. W. Norton.

———. 1961[1930]. *Civilization and Its Discontents*. Translated and edited by James Strachey. New York: W.W. Norton.

———. 1959. *Beyond The Pleasure Principle*. New York: Liveright.

———. 1919. "The Uncanny." In *The Standard Edition of the Complete Psychological Works of Sigmund Freud*, 24 vols. London: Hogarth Press, 1955, 17: 217–252. All quotations from this article are taken from the corrected reprint of this edition in *Sigmund Freud, Art and Literature*, The Pelican Freud Library, vol. 14, edited by Albert Dickson. Harmondsworth: Penguin Books, 1985, 335–376.

Freyd, J. Jennifer. 1996. *Betrayal Trauma: The Logic of Forgetting Childhood Abuse*. Cambridge: Harvard University Press.

Fuss, Diana. 1995. *Identification Papers*. New York: Routledge.

Gallop, Jane. 1995. *Pedagogy: The Question of Impersonation*. Bloomington: Indiana University Press.

——— (ed). 1985. *Reading Lacan*. Ithaca, NY: Cornell University Press.

Garrison, Jim. 1997. *Dewey and Eros: Wisdom and Desire in the Art of Teaching*. New York: Teachers College Press.

George, Hume Diana. 1988. "Anne Sexton's Suicide Poems." In *Anne Sexton: Telling the Tale*, edited by Steven E. Colburn. Ann Arbor: University of Michigan Press.

Gilmore, Leigh. 2001. *The Limits of Autobiography: Trauma, Testimony, Theory*. Ithaca, NY: Cornell University Press.

———. 1994a. "Policing Truth: Confession, Gender, and Autobiographical Authority." In *Autobiography and Postmodernism*, edited by Kathleen Ashley, Leigh Gilmore, and Gerald Peters, Amherst: University of Massachusetts Press.

———. 1994b. "The Mark of Autobiography: Postmodernism, Autobiography, and Genre." In *Autobiography and Postmodernism*, edited by Kathleen Ashley, Leigh Gilmore, and Gerald Peters, Amherst, University of Massachusetts Press. 54–78.

Goffman, Irving. 1981. "The Lecture." In *Forms of Talk*, edited by Philadelphia: University of Pennsylvania Press. 160–196.

Gill, Joanna "'My Sweeney, Mr. Eliot': Anne Sexton and The Impersonal theory of Poetry.'" Journal of Modern Literature Volume 27. number ½, Fall, 2003. pp. 36–56.

Grumet, Madeleine. 1995. "Scholae Personae: Masks for Meaning." In *Pedagogy: The Question of Impersonation*, edited by Jane Gallop. Bloomington: Indiana University Press.

Grunberger, Bela. 1989. *New Essays on Narcissism*. Edited and translated by David Macey. London: Free Association Books.

Haaken, Janice. 1998. *The Pillar of Salt: Gender, Memory and the Politics of Looking Back*. New Brunswick, NJ: Rutgers University Press.

Hassoun, Jacques. 1997. *The Cruelty of Depression: On Melancholy*. Reading, MA: Addison-Wesley.

Heilbrun, Carolyn G. 1988. *Writing a Woman's Life*. New York: Ballantine Books.

Hejinian, Lynn. 1991. "The Person and Description," *Poetics Journal* 9: 170.

Herman, Judith. 1992. *Trauma and Recovery: The Aftermath of Violence—From Domestic Abuse to Political Terror.* New York: Basic Books.

Holmes, John. 1960. *Writing Poetry.* Boston: Writer, Inc.

hooks, bell. 1994. *Teaching to Transgress: Education as the Practice of Freedom.* New York: Routledge.

Irigary, Luce. 1985. *Speculum of the Other Woman.* Translated by Gillian C. Gill, 101–103. Ithaca, NY: Cornell University Press.

Isserman, M., and Kazin, M. 1999. *America Divided: The Civil War of the 1960's.* New York: Oxford University Press.

Kant, Immanuel. 1966. *Critique of Pure Reason.* Translated by F. Max Muller. Garden City, NJ: Doubleday.

Kavaler-Adler, Susan. 2000. *The Compulsion to Create: Women Writers and Their Demon Lovers.* New York: Other Press.

Kelly, Ursula. 2004. "The Place of Reparation: Love, Loss, Ambivalence and Teaching." In *Teaching, Learning and Loving: Reclaiming Passion in Educational Practice,* edited by Daniel Liston and Jim Garrison. New York and London: Routledge. pp 153–168

Kevles, Barbara. 1972. "An Interview with Anne Sexton." *Paris Review* 160–191. This interview is reprinted as "The Art of Poetry: Anne Sexton," in *Anne Sexton: The Artists and Her Critics,* edited by J. D. McClatchy. Bloomington: Indiana University Press. pp 3–29

———. 1976. "The Dying of a Poet." *The Village Voice,* 5 April.

———. 1974. "The Art of Poetry: Anne Sexton." In *Writers at Work: The Paris Review Interviews, Fourth Series,* edited by George Plimpton, 397–424. New York: Viking.

Kirsch, Gesa E. and Jey S. Ritchie, 1995. "Beyond The Personal: Theorizing A Politics of Location in Composition Research." In CCC 46.1 pp. 7–29

Klein, Melanie. 1961. *Narrative of a Child Analysis: The Conduct of The Psycho-Analysis of Children of a Ten-Year-Old Boy.* London: Hogarth Press.

Kristeva, Julia. 1989. *Black Sun: Depression and Melancholia.* Translated by Leon S. Roudiez. New York: Columbia University Press.

———. 1987. *In the Beginning Was Love: Psychoanalysis and Faith.* Translated by Arthur Goldhammer. New York: Columbia UP.

———. 1983. *Tales of Love.* Transated by Leon S. Roudiez. New York: Columbia University Press.

———. 1980. *Powers of Horror: An Essay on Abjection.* Translated by Leon S. Roudiez. New York: Columbia University Press.

Kumin, Maxine. 1981. Preface. In *Anne Sexton: Complete Poems.* Boston: Houghton Mifflin.

Lacan, Jacques. 1978. "The Eye and the Gaze." In *The Four Fundamental Concepts of Psychoanalysis,* edited by Jacques-Alaain Miller, translated by Alan Sheridan. New York: W. W. Norton.

———. 1977. *Ecrits: A Selection.* New York: WW. Norton. & Company, Inc.

———. 1968. *The Language of the Self.* Translated by Anthony Wilden. New York: Dell.

———. 1962. Unpublished seminar, "L'Angoisse," 19 December.

La Capra, Dominick. 2004. *History in Transit: Experience, Identity, Critical Theory.* Ithaca, NY: Cornell University Press.

———. 2001. "Writing History, Writing Trauma." In *Writing and Revising the Disciplines,* edited by Jonathan Monroe. Ithaca, NY: Cornell University Press.

———. 1999. "Trauma, Absence, Loss." *Critical Inquiry* 24(4).

———. 1997. "From What Subject-Position(s) Should One Address the Politics of Research?" In *The Politics of Research,* edited by E. Ann Kaplan and George Levine, 59–68. New Brunswick, NJ: Rutgers University Press.

Leonard, Linda. 1989. *Witness to the Fire: Creativity and the Veil of Addiction.* New York: Shambhala Publications.

McClatchy, J.D. (ed.). 1978. *Anne Sexton: The Artist and Her Critics.* Bloomington: Indiana University Press.

Middlebrook, Diane Wood. 1991. *Anne Sexton: A Biography.* New York: Houghton Mifflin.

———. 1988. "Poet of Weird Abundance." In *Anne Sexton: Telling the Tale,* edited by Steven E. Colburn, 447–470. Ann Arbor: University of Michigan Press.

———. 1985. "I Tapped My Own Head: The Apprenticeship of Anne Sexton." In *Coming to Light: American Women Poets in the Twentieth Century,* edited by Diane Wood Middlebrook and Marilyn Yalom. Ann Arbor: University of Michigan Press.

Middlebrook, Diane Wood, and Diana Hume, George (eds). 1988. *Selected Poems of Anne Sexton.* New York: Houghton Mifflin.

Miller, Jacques-Alain. 1988. "Extimite." *Prose Studies* 11(December): 121–130.

Miller, Janet L. 2005. *The Sounds of Silence Breaking: Women, Autobiography and Curriculum.* New York. Peter Lang.

Miller, Nancy K. 1991. *Getting Personal: Feminist Occasions and Other Autobiographical Acts.* New York and London: Routledge.

Miller, Richard. 1996. "The Nervous System." *College English* 58(3): 265–286.

Mills, Charles W. 1997. *The Racial Contract.* Ithaca, NY: Cornell University Press.

Moi, Toril. 1999. *What Is a Woman?: And Other Essays.* London: Oxford University Press.

Morrison, Toni. 1990. *Playing in the Dark: Whiteness and the Literary Imagination.* New York: Vintage.

Oliver, K. 1993. *Reading Kristeva: Unraveling the Double-bind.* Bloomington: Indiana University Press.

Ong, Walter J. 2002. *Orality and Literacy.* New York: Routledge.

———. 1981. *Fighting for Life: Contest, Sexuality, and Consciousness.* Ithaca, NY: Cornell University Press.

Orner, Mimi. 1993. "Interrupting the Calls for Student Voice in "Liberatory" Education: A Feminist Poststructuralist Perspective." In *Feminisms and Critical Pedagogy,* edited by Carmen Luke and Jennifer Gore, 74–89. New York: Routledge.

Ostriker, Alicia S. 2005. *Writing Like a Woman.* Ann Arbor: University of Michigan Press.

———. 1988. "That Story: The Changes of Anne Sexton." In *Anne Sexton: Telling the Tale,* edited by Steven E. Colburn. Ann Arbor: University of Michigan Press.

———. 1982. "That Story: Anne Sexton and Her Transformations." *The American Poetry Review* (July/August): 11–14.

Otte, George. 1995. "In-voicing: Beyond the Voice Debate." In *Pedagogy: The Question of Impersonation,* edited by Jane Gallop. Bloomington: Indiana University Press. pp. 147–154

Pagano, JoAnne. 1991. "Moral Fictions: The Dilemma of Theory and Practice." In *Stories Lives Tell: Narrative and Dialogue in Education,* edited by C. Witherall and N. Noddings, 193–206. New York: Teachers College Press.

———. 1990. *Exiles and Communities: Teaching in the Patriarchal Wilderness.* Albany: State University of New York Press.

Perloff, Marjorie. 1999. "Language Poetry and the Lyric Subject: Ron Silliman's Albany, Susan Howe's Buffalo." *Critical Inquiry* 25(3): 405.

Pennebaker, James W., and Sandra Klihr Beall. (1986) "Confronting a Traumatic Event: Toward an Understanding of Inhibition and Disease." *Journal of Abnormal Psychology* 95, no. 3 274–81.

Phelan, Peggy. 1993. *Unmarked: The Politics of Performance.* London: Routledge.

———. 1996.

Phillips, Adam. 1996. *On Flirtation: Psychoanalytic Essays on the Uncommited Life.* Cambridge, MA: Harvard University Press.

———. 1994. *On Kissing, Tickling and Being Bored: Psychoanalytic Essays on the Unexamined Life,* Cambridge: Harvard University Press.

———. 1988. *Winnicott.* Cambridge: Harvard University Press.

Pinar, William. 1988. "Autobiography and the Architecture of the Self." *Journal of Curriculum Theorizing* 8(1): 7–36.

Pitt, Alice. 2006. "Mother Love's Education." In *Love's Return: Psychoanalytic Essays on Childhood, Teaching and Learning.* NY Routledge pp. 87–105.

Probyn, Elspeth. 1996. *Outside Belongings.* New York: Routledge.

Rashkin, Esther. 1988. "Tools for a New Psychoanalytic Literary Criticism, *Diacritics* (Winter) pp. 31–52.

———. 1992. *Family Secrets and the Psychoanalysis of Narrative.* Princeton: Princeton University Press.

Readings, Bill. 1996. *The University in Ruins.* Cambridge: Harvard University Press.

Edited by Mary Rhiel and David Suchoff Rhiel, Mary. 1996. *The Seductions of Biography.* Boston: Routledge.

Russo, Mary. 1994. *The Female Grotesque: Risk, Excess and Modernity.* New York: Routledge.

Schechtner, Richard. 1985. *Between Theatre and Anthropology.* Philadelphia: University of Pennsylvania Press.

Sandoval, Chela. 2000. *Methodology of the Oppressed.* Minneapolis: University of Minnesota Press.

Scarry, Elaine. 1985. *The Body in Pain: The Making and Unmaking of the World.* Oxford: Oxford University Press.

Salvio, Paula M. 1999. "Reading in the Age of Testimony." In *Building Moral Communities Through Educational Drama,* edited by Betty Jane Wagner. London: Greenwood.

Salvio, Paula M. "Reading in the Age of Testimony" in B.J. Wagner (Editor) *Building Moral Communities through Educational Drama* (pp. 39–62). Ablex Publishing, Stamford, CT.

Sexton, Anne. 1988a. "Consorting with Angels." In *Selected Poems if Anne Sexton,* edited by Diane Wood Middlebrook and Diana Hume George. Boston: Houghton Mifflin.

————. 1988b. "For John Who Begs Me Not to Inquire Further." In *Selected Poems of Anne Sexton*, edited by Diane Wood Middlebrook and Diana Hume George. Boston: Houghton Mifflin.

————. 1988c. "Lullaby." In *Selected Poems of Anne Sexton*, edited by Diane Wood Middlebrook and Diana Hume George. Boston: Houghton Mifflin.

————. 1988d. "Old." In *Selected Poems of Anne Sexton*, edited by Diane Wood Middlebrook and Diana Hume George. Boston: Houghton Mifflin.

————. 1981. "Two Sons" and "Man and Wife." In *The Complete Poems: Anne Sexton*. Boston: Houghton Mifflin.

————. 1974. *The Death Notebooks*. Boston: Houghton Mifflin.

————. 1969. *Love Poems*. New York: Houghton Mifflin.

————. 1966. *Live or Die*. New York: Houghton Mifflin.

————. 1962. *All My Pretty Ones*. New York: Houghton Mifflin.

————. 1960. *To Bedlam and Part Way Back*. New York: Houghton Mifflin.

Sexton, Linda Gray. 1994. *Searching for Mercy Street: My Journey Back to My Mother, Anne Sexton*. Boston: Little Brown.

Sexton, Linda Gray, and Lois Ames (eds). 1977. *Anne Sexton: A Self-Portrait in Letters*. Boston: Houghton Mifflin.

Silin, Jonathan G. 1995. *Sex, Death and the Education of Children: Our Passion for Ignorance in the Age of Aids*. New York and London: Teachers College Press.

Skorczewski, Dawn. 1996. "What Prison Is This?: Literary Critics Cover Incest in Anne Sexton's 'Briar Rose.'" *Signs: Journal of Women, Culture and Society* 21(Winter): 309–342.

Smith, Sidonie. 1987. *A Poetics of Women's Autobiography: Marginality and the Fictions of Self-Representation*. Bloomington: Indiana University Press.

Stallybrass, Peter, and Allon White. 1986. *The Politics and Poetics of Transgression*. Ithaca, NY: Cornell University Press.

Stanislavski, Constantin. 1945. *Building a Character*. New York: Theatre Arts Books.

Steedman, Carolyn. 1987. *Landscape for a Good Woman: A Story of Two Lives*. New Brunswick, NJ: Rutgers University Press.

Steedman, Carolyn Kaye. 1992. "History and Autobiography: Different Pasts." in *Past Tenses: Essays on Writing Autobiography and History*. London: Rivers Oram. Pp. 41–50.

Suchoff, David, and Mary Rhiel (eds). 1996. *The Seductions of Biography*. New York: Routledge.

Sumara, Dennis. *Private Readings in Public: Schooling the Literary Imagination*. New York: Peter Lang. 1996.

Talburt, Susan. 1999. *Subject to Identity: Sexuality and Academic Practices in Higher Education*. Albany: State University of New York Press.

Talburt, Susan, and Paula Salvio. 2004. "The Personal Professor . . ." In *Imagining Higher Education: The Academy in Popular Culture*, edited by Susan Edgerton. New York: Routledge. pp 17–38.

Taubman, Peter 1997. "Autobiography Without a Self." Paper presented at the American Educational Research Association, Chicago.

Taubman, Peter M. 2006 "I Love Them To Death." In *Love's Return: Psychoanalytic Essays on Childhood, Teaching and Learning*. ed. By Gail M. Boldt and Paula M. Salvio New York: Routledge. pp. 19–32.

————. 1990. "Achieving the Right Distance." *Educational Theory* 4(1): 121–133.

Tobin, Lad. 2003. *Reading Student Writing.* Portsmouth, NH: Heinemann.

Todd, Sharon. 2003. *Learning from the Other: Levinas, Psychoanalysis, and Ethical Possibilities in Education.* Albany: State University of New York Press.

Tompson Taylor, Lisa, and Gray Mary Ford. 1991. Letter to the *New York Times.*

Vidler, Anthony. 1992. *The Architectural Uncanny: Essays in the Modern Unhomely.* Cambridge: Massachusetts Institute of Technology.

Walcott, Rinaldo. 2005. "Land to Light On?: Making Reparation in a Time of Transnationality." Paper presented at Wilfrid Laurier University, Waterloo Ontario, Canada, Conference entitled *Beyond Autoethnography: Writing Race and Ethnicity in Canada.*

Walkerdine, Valerie. 1990. *Schoolgirl Fictions.* London: Verso.

————. 2000. "Violent Boys and Precocious Girls: Regulating Children at the End of the Millennium." In Critical Issues in Early Childhood 1 (1) 3–22.

Warnock, Tilly. 1997. "Language and Literature as Equipment for Living: Revision as a Life Skill." In *Writing and Healing: Toward an Informed Practice,* edited by Charles M. Anderson and Marian M. MacCurdy. Urbana-Champagne: NCTE. pp 34–57.

Williams, Patricia. 1991. *The Alchemy of Race and Rights: Diary of a Law Professor.* Cambridge: Harvard University Press.

Winnicott, Donald. 1987. *Babies and Their Mothers*: London: Free Association Press.

————. 1969. "The Uses of an Object." *Introduction to Journal of Psychoanalysis* 50: 711–716.

————. 1965. *The Maturational Process and the Facilitating Environment.* New York: International University Press.

————. 1958. *Collected Papers: Through Paediatrics to Psycho-Analysis.* London: Tavistock.

Woolf, Virginia. 1976. "A Sketch from the Past." In *Moments of Being: Unpublished Autobiographical Writings,* edited by Jeanne Schulkind,. 69. New York: Hogarth Press.

Zeiger, Melissa F. 1997. *Beyond Consolation: Death, Sexuality, and the Changing Shapes of Elegy.* Ithaca, NY, and London: Cornell University Press.

Index

sanity-health struggle, 15
sarcasm, 37
Scarry, Elaine, 27
Schopenhauer, Arthur, 70
scientific inquiry, 25
*Searching for Mercy Street: My Journey
    Back to My Mother* (Sexton),
    44, 82
secret's inhered from a person's earlier
    history, 13
self
    lost sense of, 12
    "true" *vs.* false, 85
self-awareness, 54
self-deception, 9, 52, 53, 55, 61, 103, 109
self-disclosure
    in Sexton's poems, 56
    in teaching, 3
self-documentation, 17
self-estrangement, 100
self-evacuation, 12
self-forgetting, 53–54
self-image
    narcissistic in teaching, 8–9
    of Sexton, 115
self-insight, 31
self-pity, 3
self-punishment, 10
self-regard, 113
self-representation, 90–91, 98, 102
sense of order, from self-disclosure, 54
sentimentality, 8
Sexton, Alfred Muller II ("Kayo"), 1, *73*,
    80, 81–82, 83
Sexton, Joyce Ladd ("Joy"), *80*, 81, 83, 95
Sexton, Linda Gray, 17, 38, 98
    incest and, 83–84, 89–90
    photos of, *78, 79, 80*
    relationship with mother, 2, 44,
        82–83, 95
sexual abuse, 83–85
    eradication of identity and, 22
    incest (*See* incest)
    molestation, 112
    as poetry theme, 22, 23
sexual desire, 19–20

sexuality, female, 52
shame, 52
Shelley prize, 2
Shot in the Heart (Gilmore), 26
Simpson, Louis, 36
"Six Boys Who Were Drafted from
    Brooklyn" (Paley), 112–113
skepticism, 25, 88
Snodgrass, W.D., 36, 37, 52
social involvements, 33
social order, 38
social space, 44
social subjectivity, in classroom, 55
"Somewhere in Africa" (Sexton), 19
Stallybrass, Peter, 10, 39
Stanislavski, Constantin, 29
Starbuck, George, 51, 52, 56, 59, 63, 69, 97
Steedman, Carolyn, 5, 62–63
strategies, *vs.* tactics, 39
students, Sexton's
    Batten, Pricilla, 109–112
    incorporation of teacher, 42
    Leverich, Chris, 18–19, 20, 22, 23,
        28, 33
    past associations of, 13–14
student-teacher relationship
    boundaries of, 44–45
    recognition in, 109
    Sexton and, 8, 33, *74*
subordination, 71
suffering, personal, 21, 25–26, 89
suicidal themes, 52
suicide, 24
    of Anne Sexton, 81
    as poetry theme, 56, 57
    teacher, deomon, artist mother, 6
suicide attempts, 2, 93–94, 96

tactics, pedagogical
    in daily life, 39
    mimetic, 48
    narrative, 40
    Sexton's use of, 47–49, 98, 99
    vs. strategies, 11, 39
talking circle, "hidden curriculum of," 64
tautology, 116

teacher/teachers. *See also* student-teacher
   relationship
   as actor, 102
   "good-enough," 83, 98, 102
   loss of meaning and, 7
   Sexton as, 6, 49, 100
   strategies to recover from narcisstic
     wounds, 61
Teachers and Writers Collaborative, 2, 99,
   103, 104, 106, 112
teaching
   as consolation for loss, 26
   learning and, 42–43
   of literature, lack of black America
     in curriculum, 107–108
   methods, for poetry revision, 8
   normative view, insufficiency of, 6
   performative approach to, 31–32, 34
   place of personal in, 3
   recognition in, 109
   as reparation, 99–102
   self-disclosure in, 3
   strategies/tactics, 11
teaching journals, Sexton, 103–104, 107,
   109, 112, 116, 121
teaching life, Sexton's, 2–3, 11, 14–15, 18
   ambivalence in, 31, 49
   the Other and, 104
   pedagogy of reparation and,
     101–102
   troubled aspects of, 23–24
   vulnerable dimensions of, 104
tight lyric form, 22
To Bedlam and Part Way Back (Sexton),
   37, 52, 56, 57, 61, 68, 70
Tobin, Lad, 113
Tompson, Lisa Taylor, 86–87
Torok, Maria, 13, 19–20
"total immersion of you into subject,"
   27
traditional forms, value of, 22
trauma. *See also* incest; sexual abuse
   double-meaning of, 84
   family, 101
   historical conditions of, 22–23
   learning and, 85–86

performative pedagogies, 31–32
stability/reliability of narratives on,
   86, 87
"tricks." *See* tactics, pedagogical
"true self," 91, 94, 96
truth, 45, 54, 88–89, 101, 116
"The Truth the Dead Know" (Sexton),
   19
Tufts University, Anne Sexton at, 77
"Two Sons" (Sexton), 92–93

uncanny, sense of, 11–12, 14, 45, 100
unconscious father concept, 65–69
The University in Ruins (Readings), 7
"Unknown Girl in the Maternity Ward"
   (Sexton), 95–96

victimization, 98
voice, 5

Walcott, Rinaldo, 98
Wayland High School, Wayland, Mas-
   sachussetts, 2, 99, 103, 105, 106,
   113, 114
"weird abundance," 6, 11, 15, 117
White, Allon, 10, 39
white supremacy, 106–108, 114
Williams, Patricia, 21, 119
Winnicott, D.W.
   disregard for subjectivity of moth-
     ers, 92
   "good-enough" mother concept, 83,
     91, 92
   "true self," 85
women
   American middle-class, 1
   biological facts of womanhood,
     36–37
   images of, 9–10 (*See also* female
     bodies)
   love between, 58
   trust and, 64
women writers, 64
Woolf, Virginia, 9, 120
"workshop method." *See* poetry
   workshops